STO

The church basement fills up early. Truck drivers in overalls and teachers in shirts and ties, young men with kinky hair down their backs and old women with shawls over their heads, nuns in black habits, priests in clerical collars and ministers in turtleneck sweaters, all greet one another with a hug and kiss and then scramble for a seat. Then it begins. Singing. Praying. Silence. Testimony. More singing. An hour and a half after the last song people are sweeping up the floor and putting the chairs away, and the last knots of individuals are gently asked to head homeward so the rented building can be locked up.

All across the country this scene is repeated as Christians of many churches are becoming more deeply aware of the Holy Spirit and are forming prayer communities capable of revitalizing contemporary Christianity. In FILLED WITH NEW WINE, James W. Jones contends that the rediscovery of the Spirit need not lead to a new sectarianism but affords a unique opportunity for church growth and renewal, especially in the mainline Protestant and Roman Catholic traditions. This book is written for the members of those churches who up till now may have been put off by certain aspects of the charismatic movement—overemotionalism, anti-intellectualism, exaggerated individualism—but who are interested in the place of the movement itself in the total life of the church.

Dr. Jones begins with a colorful description of the life of one charismatic community and concludes with a discussion of the movement's relevance to some concrete problems of church renewal. The intention throughout is to show that the charismatic experience is ordered to the formation of Christian com-

(Continued on back flap)

punctuate his discussion, make it practical and timely, and underscore his belief that the charismatic movement, if properly understood, is the one movement that can effectively renew all the churches.

FILLED

WITH NEW WINE

The Charismatic Renewal
of the Church

JAMES W. JONES

Harper & Row, Publishers
New York, Evanston, San Francisco, London

FIRST EDITION

Designed by C. Linda Dingler

Library of Congress Cataloging in Publication Data
Jones, James William, 1943–
    Filled with new wine.
    Includes bibliographical references.
    1. Pentecostalism. 2. Church renewal. I. Title.
BX8763.J65   262'.001   73–6342
ISBN 0–06–064187–5

1783508

To Emily

Pour out the wine, Lord, pour out the wine,
We are the branch and you are the vine,
You are the one who loves us all the time,
We just say, "Amen, Lord, pour out the wine."
                                        —Pentecostal hymn

Jesus said, "No one pours new wine into old wineskins.
If they do, the skins split, the wine runs out, and the
skins are ruined. New wine is for new wineskins so that
both are kept intact."
                                        —Matthew 9:17

What we have in the church today is plenty of new
    wineskins
and no new wine to pour into them.
                                        —Anonymous

CONTENTS

PREFACE

Spiritual renewal is in. Churches pass resolutions calling for a deeper spiritual life. The media feature stories on superspiritual Jesus freaks. Books on Pentecostalism sell. Seminary students ask for classes in spirituality. Who could have predicted it? Some years ago it was the theology of revolution and social change that captured the public eye. Then the slogan "God Is Dead" resounded in the media. Now one hears churches crying out for spiritual renewal. Like a man drunk on the strong wine of cultural change, modern theology has staggered from one side of the road to the other. Torn loose from any anchor, churches, theologians, and religious pundits have been blown around by every breeze that has swept through the society.

Pentecostalism, or the charismatic movement, was here long before spiritual renewal became a mini-fad in the churches and will be going on long after the popular mood changes again. But at this time, when many express a concern for renewal, it is important for the churches to consider the movement afresh. Many in the traditional churches are perplexed by what they read about Pentecostals; many are turned off by what they hear. This book is written for just such an audience. It is an introduction to the charismatic movement for people who are in the major Christian traditions and who may have been put off by Pentecostalism.

As an Episcopal clergyman who has been involved in various aspects of the movement for several years I am convinced that, properly understood, it will lead to a renewal of the churches rather than to schisms within them. Although rejecting some aspects of Pentecostalism and critical of it, I remain involved. The conviction that impels me to write is that the charismatic movement is *the* movement that can renew the churches, if they are open to it.

Being a professor of history and theology as well as a priest, I feel that the churches must not only experience renewal but also reflect upon and come to understand it. What is needed is not merely a description of Pentecostal experience but also a practical theology of church renewal based on the charismatic movement. This is important not only for those involved in charismatic activity or interested in learning more about it. Persons concerned with practical revival of the church or the theology of religious life and experience can all learn from the charismatics.

My approach to Pentecostalism was developed in the course of many talks given to Episcopal, Catholic, and Reformed church audiences. Pulled together for a 1972 Lenten series on "Life in the Spirit" at Trinity Episcopal Church in Princeton, New Jersey, these ideas reached their present form as lectures for a lay school of religion at St. Mark's Episcopal Parish, New Canaan, Connecticut. To give some flavor of the process behind the writing, I have included some of the questions asked after each talk by the people of St. Mark's.

I would not have written anything without the help of the Rev. James R. Whittemore, Rector of Trinity Church, Princeton, and the Rev. Dr. Grant A. Morrill, Rector of St. Mark's Parish, New Canaan. They encouraged me to develop a series on the charismatic movement which would be useful for people in the major church traditions. Their wise counsel and generous and gracious support often helped overcome my discouragement with the project. To them and the people of their parishes I owe a deep debt of gratitude. The superb work of Ms. Helene Schnurbush and the staff of St. Mark's Parish transformed my speaker's notes into a viable manuscript and provided a transcript of the discussion so that I could use people's questions as part of the book. I am especially thankful for their efforts. Sandra K. Jones shared many of the experiences that made this work possible, helpfully read the manuscript, and encouraged me in the many speaking engagements in which the material was refined.

No one can teach who has not first been taught, and I am grateful to the people of the St. Paul the Apostle Prayer Community in the Twin Cities of Minnesota and the Cenacle House Prayer Community in New Jersey who taught me about the work of the Spirit.

Most English translations of the New Testament in this book are the responsibility of the author. A few have been taken from the Revised Standard Version.

As this manuscript was being conceived, our first child, Emily, was born and to her this work is affectionately dedicated.

FILLED WITH NEW WINE

WHAT IS THE SPIRIT DOING?

In the church there is a longing to get back to the experiences that lie at the heart of the Christian faith. During the last few years my family and I have lived in three different parts of the country: New England, Minnesota, and now New Jersey. In all three places I came to know both clergy and laymen and detected a deep hunger in many of them—hunger for the basic experiences of Christianity and the renewal of the church. I have also been asked to speak about the work of the Spirit before various congregations and have been surprised at their openness and interest in this topic.

At the university I am confronted with the same concerns. As a teacher I work too closely with young people to be overly romantic about the youth culture. But if, as is often said, young people are the seismographs of society, then what is happening in the church is a tremor symptomatic of something happening throughout the culture. Many young persons are searching for a renewal of the basic experiences of life and faith. This drive, which has overpopulated our university courses in religion, has taken some back to nature, others deep into the contemplative cells of Eastern religions or down into the depths of drug-induced consciousness. In all this one sees a strong impulse to get down to the experiential roots of what we say and do and believe.

Even in scholarly circles religious experience has become a permissible topic of conversation. Friends of mine who teach in seminaries tell me that seminarians are suddenly interested in courses on prayer and meditation. What, if anything, will be the result of it all I am in no position to say; too many fads have come and gone both in the church and the society. The most important aspect of the trend, I believe, is the concern on the part of laymen and clergyman that the Christian faith come alive in the life of the church. This is not simply a pietistic longing for private, inward excitement. For most it is a thirst not only for personal renewal but also for the revitalization of the church. It involves the movements for a deeper sense of community in the congregation, for a liturgy that will bring the everyday life of people into the sanctuary without losing the sense of the majesty of God, and for a church that will provide guidance in the great social and political ferment of the day without either running from the world into hothouses of piety or imposing on the world the man-made ideologies of right or left.

I want to describe something of what the Spirit is doing to provide the renewal God's people cry out for. God loves His church; He has not left it in its apparent weakness. This is an exciting time to be a Christian and to be involved, for the power of God is abroad in the land. He is at work to awaken the basic religious life of individuals and to reawaken the church as the community of Christ. The question is not whether the church will be renewed. Of course it will be; the Spirit is at work. The only question is whether you and I will prove a hindrance or a channel to God's activity.

To renew, as the word implies, is not to create out of nothing, but rather to revitalize what has always been there. When I speak of the spiritual renewal of the church I do not imply that the Spirit is somehow gone from it and has to be reintroduced. The Spirit has never been absent from the church. However, at times the church's awareness appears dim, and the attention it gives to the Spirit is consequently lessened. Right after the day of Pentecost the early church was keenly aware of the Spirit. Examining the evidence of that time may give a clue as to what life in the Spirit might be like and what happens when people are responsive to it.

St. Paul describes spiritual life in the primitive Christian assemblies as follows:

There are varieties of gifts but the same Spirit, and there are different ministries but the same Lord, and there are different functions but the same God is functioning through all of them. To each one is given a manifestation of the Spirit for the common good. To one the Spirit gives a word of wisdom, to another He gives a word of knowledge, to another faith, to another the gift of healing, to another the working of miracles, to another prophecy . . . to another various kinds of languages [or "tongues"], to another the translation [or "interpretation"] of these languages. In all of these the same Spirit is at work distributing to each one the gifts He wants him to have. A body is one entity with many members, and all the members of the body, although there are many, make up a single body. So it is with Christ. Through the one Spirit we were all baptized into the one body . . . where we were all given the same Spirit to drink. For the body does not consist of one member but many. . . . You are the body of Christ and each of you is one of the members. And God has appointed in His church apostles, prophets, teachers, miracle-workers, healers, helpers, administrators, speakers in various languages. [1 Cor. 12]

From this passage we learn several things about life in the early church. First, the Spirit was vividly known. The first chapter of the present volume describes a modern community where experience of the Spirit is equally vivid and discusses how this can rekindle the church.

We also learn from Paul that the Spirit made its presence known in the early assemblies and the lives of people through what Paul calls "gifts," such as speaking God's word, working

miracles and miraculous healings, and speaking and interpreting unknown languages. The term Paul uses for these gifts is the
Greek word *charismata;* thus the movement for renewal in the
church through a restoring of these various gifts of the Spirit is '
called the charismatic movement. The first charismatic movement in fact created the church on the day of Pentecost, and
I shall analyze part of the meaning of this event. Discussion of
the rediscovery of spiritual gifts in the Pentecostal movement
will include some account of how the modern Pentecostals imposed their own interpretation on their new experience of the
Spirit. Similarly, tracing the spread of Pentecostalism into the
mainline Protestant churches will involve an explanation of
how this "neo-Pentecostal" movement got into trouble. Bringing this biography of the Spirit up to date will mean considering
the experience in the Catholic Church and how these charismatic Catholics have found ways of understanding the gifts of
the Spirit that previous Pentecostals overlooked.

The charismatic movement has produced considerable controversy, and in this book I shall face some of the theological
objections and psychological analyses that have been hurled at
the Pentecostals. Consideration of these arguments will help
clarify the various types of gifts, their meaning, and why they
are considered so important.

The average congregation today is not a unified body; rather
it usually contains a spectrum of commitment ranging from a
small band of hard-working enthusiasts through those who attend church with uninspired diligence to those standing on the
steps debating with themselves whether to enter. The relevance of the charismatic encounter with the Spirit for these
various groups within the modern church will be a part of our
concern. This type of encounter, apparently so natural to people in the early church, does not come easily today. Some of the
practical problems of experiencing in modern society the same
gifts Paul takes for granted in the first Christian meetings are

analyzed here and their importance for Christian morality discussed.

Finally, the passage from Paul's letter cited above reflects the fact that the spiritual life of the primitive church took place in a community where members were as close to each other as your hand is to your foot. I have tried to sketch a contemporary theology of Christian community. In his letters to the Ephesians and Colossians Paul says that the plan of God is to fill creation with His presence—to be "all in all." How does God intend to accomplish this? In Ephesians Paul says it is destined to be accomplished through "gifts" to mankind (Eph. 4), and the gifts he lists are very similar to the spiritual gifts he speaks of in this passage to the Corinthians. In both the Corinthian and Ephesian letters Paul says the purpose of spiritual gifts is to form believers into community—or, as he says, to build up the body of Christ. When the disciples were filled with the Spirit on the day of Pentecost, and thus gathered into a community from which in turn the same Spirit flowed into others, the divine purpose to fill all things was being carried forward. I have tried in this book to explain the nature of Christian community and its significance in carrying out God's intention for His creation; also some of the concrete ways in which it is essential for a mature life in the Spirit, and sundry practical issues that surround the formation of Christian community.

Most people's experience of that community (whatever it may be) comes through the church. My last chapter applies basic insights about the Christian life which arise out of the charismatic movement to the problems of church renewal. Various movements for church renewal are analyzed to see why they have failed to renew the church while accomplishing a great deal of good in other areas. I shall argue that such programs will always prove self-defeating and counterproductive to their goal of renewal. On the other hand, some of the concrete ways in which the charismatic movement can be a renewal of the church are explored. For it does not aim at rekindling the individual's experience of the Spirit as an end in itself, but rather so that the whole church may be invigorated. Nor does the movement even aim at awakening the church as an end in itself, but rather—and only—so that the church can be a better instrument of God's plan for the world He has created. In conclusion we shall find, I hope, some hint of the centrality of the charismatic movement for the recreation of the world.

Chapter 1

LIFE IN THE SPIRIT

Living in Charismatic Community

The church basement fills up early. In order to get a seat people begin appearing a half hour before the meeting starts. Truck drivers in overalls and teachers in shirts and ties, young men with kinky hair down their backs and old women with shawls over their heads, nuns in black habits and nuns in miniskirts, priests in clerical collars and ministers in turtleneck sweaters, all greet one another with a hug and kiss and then scramble for a seat. People are throwing their arms around each other, waving their hands in excitement as they talk, or listening quietly with their faces rapt in concentration. The chairs are arranged in concentric circles so that everyone faces the center, and over four hundred of these chairs have been filled. Adults are standing around the perimeter of the room while young people sit cross-legged on the remaining floor space.

Singing starts, led by three persons in the center of the circle with guitars. People clap loudly and exchange bright-eyed smiles with those around them. "We are one in the Spirit, we are one in the Lord," the song says. A newcomer arrives apprehensively. Overwhelmed by all the assorted humanity crowded into a rather small basement, he glances around and starts to withdraw. Someone in the outer rim of chairs offers him a seat. It is not clear whether he is going to sit in it or hide under it.

He sits down and slowly begins to clap in time with the music. Hundreds of voices, sounding as one, weave into a blanket which embraces the newcomer. The fear runs from his face and the taut spring in his back gradually uncoils. He smiles back at the people around him.

After about fifteen minutes of singing a man stands up in the center of the circle. He welcomes all the newcomers and tells them that the purpose of this gathering is to praise and worship the Father, the Son, and the Holy Spirit. He sits down. People begin softly addressing casual words of praise into the air above them. "Thank you Jesus," "Praise God," "Glory and honor to you, O heavenly Father," form a muted tapestry of thanksgiving above the crowded seats. A voice starts to chant these words of praise. Soon other voices join the chant with different harmonies swelling from different corners of the room. Some are singing in foreign languages. Everyone seems to be setting his words of praise to his own tune and in a different language, and yet it all blends together into a great motet of thanksgiving. The sound rushes higher and higher to a crescendo of intensity and then, without any external signal, quickly dies down, leaving behind an awesome silence in the densely packed room.

The stillness seems to absorb every sound and to draw the restlessness out of each person as a vacuum sucks poison from a wound, until it disintegrates under a voice which speaks of God's love in words reminiscent of the prophets of the Old Testament. " 'I am calling together my people in love,' says the Lord. Watch, listen, wait," the voice tells the assembly. One by one a few offer sentences of thanksgiving to God for sickness healed, families reunited, or insights gained. Another man stands and speaks for a few minutes on the importance of those who have taken the name Christian being brothers and sisters in community and finding ways to love and be of service to each other.

There is more silence. Each tries to tie together the threads of the meeting as they unwind—the words about God calling His people together, the song about being one in the Spirit, the speaker's words about living like brothers and sisters. Somewhere someone begins to read a passage from Paul's letter to the Ephesians, "I ask God from the wealth of his glory, to give you power through his Spirit to be strong in your inner selves, and that Christ will make his home in your hearts, through faith. I pray that you will have your roots and foundations in love and that you, together with all God's people, may have the power to understand . . . how broad and long and high and deep is Christ's love. . . ." (Eph. 3:16 ff.)

With a glow on her face, a woman stands and tells how last week her sister was taken to the hospital with both kidneys shut down and put immediately into intensive care. Fighting her way through the hospital personnel, this woman came to visit her sister and, more on impulse than in faith, put her hands upon the sick woman's body and asked God to heal her. The next day the woman was moved from intensive care, and the day after that released from the hospital, her kidneys functioning perfectly. The crowd breaks out into song. A young man with blond curly hair hiding most of his face stands and says that this is his first night at the meeting. It seems he had been in jail awaiting trial as a drug pusher. Kicked out of several clinics as beyond the reach of rehabilitation, and loitering on the street waiting to waste away or die of overdose, he was picked up by the police. One of the young people from the assembled group had gone to the jail to visit prisoners, and meeting this prisoner (being a former addict himself), struck up a conversation. The charges against the young man had been dropped for lack of evidence, and when released he sought out the boy who had visited him. He begins to tremble a bit as he relates to the group how he went to this boy's room, where they talked and then asked God to free him from the hold drugs had over him. That was two weeks earlier, and since then he has lived on the streets without any desire for narcotics. From the age of sixteen he has never gone more than three days without drugs except when he was in jail.

No sooner does the former addict sit down then a woman rises to tell how her son was in a car accident and was taken away in an ambulance, bleeding internally. She was met at the hospital by doctors in white coats and long faces who said the boy's condition was grave and they were trying to decide whether to operate. She called several members of the group, who came down to the hospital and gathered outside his room. Standing in a circle but without saying a word, they asked God's help for the injured boy. He was soon wheeled from his room for the last round of examinations, only to be wheeled back a half hour later. The doctors found no sign of internal bleeding or any reason to operate. He was removed from the critical list and sent home after a few days. The group sings another thankful song. A man stands next and relates how his house burned down and members of the group were housing him and his family, providing them meals and collecting clothes for them until they could find a new home. An elderly woman stands; in speech blurred by a thick eastern European accent she describes how she had been ill in bed and was reading the biblical accounts of Jesus' crucifixion, and suddenly saw that he was present with her in her pain because he too had experienced pain and therefore knew what it was like. She sits down. On and on it goes. For almost an hour the group is treated to accounts of people healed, marriages restored, new knowledge gained.

The man who first welcomed everyone now asks that people spend some time in silence, thinking over what has transpired. The same awesome silence settles into the basement, muffling the noise of over four hundred people pressed together. The stillness rarely breaks. Occasionally more words are spoken, reminiscent of the Old Testament prophets, about God's love for his people or the necessity of seeking His will and listening for Him. The silence is gathered together in a quiet song which tells of God's Spirit being like a fire that burns through the world in the hearts of men.

The last few minutes are spent considering various petitions. Brief sentences of concern are held before the group—"pray for my grandmother who is ill," "for a runaway teenager," "for an alcoholic," "for a man in prison," "for another man out of work"—to each the assembly responds, "Lord, hear our prayer." A final song is sung. It is a rousing song and everyone is brought to his feet, clapping and singing and finally holding the hands of the people on either side and swaying in time to the music in a single embrace of sharing.

Two hours after the first song the meeting is over, but few leave the church. The crowd disperses throughout the building. Several groups of twelve gather in church schoolrooms for teaching and discussion. Nine of the twelve are people relatively new to the meetings, while the other three—more experienced—lead a discussion of the basic points of Christianity and particularly the work of the Holy Spirit. The sessions last five or six weeks. In the first they speak of the love of God, and in the second of man's response to it. The third describes how the Holy Spirit was understood in the Bible and the history of the church. In the fourth there is no discussion; it is devoted instead to praying that each person will begin to experience a deeper awareness of the Spirit's presence. The last sessions deal with some of the practical problems of Christian living in the modern world. Everyone who is a member of the community goes through this series once to deepen his experience and understanding.

After the main meeting others gather in smaller rooms with a few friends to ask for God's help for some special difficulty. In one room a family is praying together for a relative who has left his wife and children. In another, a man has a few of his friends with him while asking God to heal him of cancer. Or individuals with a specific problem will ask another member of the community for help. They go off into other rooms in the church. The man who began the meeting with a word of welcome is talking with a woman about her doubts concerning prayer. In another room the man who spoke about being brothers and sisters is poring over a passage of scripture with someone who found it hard to understand when he read it at home. In still another room another man is confiding some of his own emotional turmoil to a woman from the community.

Most people stay in the big assembly room after the meeting. Coffee and cookies have been provided and are eagerly consumed as clumps of people catch up on the news of each other's lives. Those who have been talking and praying elsewhere gradually filter back to the assembly room, pick up their refreshments, and get involved in other conversations. An hour and a half after the last song people are sweeping up the floor and putting the chairs away, and the last straggling knots of individuals are gently asked to head homeward so the rented building can be locked up.

This weekly meeting for prayer is the center of a charismatic community's life, but most of the people see other members of the community during the rest of the week as well. It draws from many different churches; all members are active both in their own church and in this community of prayer that meets during the week. Thus they may see each other on Sunday as well as at the meeting on Thursday evenings. Usually several members live in the same neighborhood and meet in local gatherings to read the Bible and pray. When problems develop, they call others of the community for help. Some women who are at home during the day maintain contact with certain people by phone. One group visits prisons, another works with runaway teenagers. Men from the community meet for lunch or on the weekends to help each other with work around their homes. Thus the spiritual experience of the prayer meeting takes form in the family, the neighborhood, the city, and the factory.

About a dozen of its men and women meet every week or so to coordinate the common life. Since the group is not connected with any congregation, it rents the basement of a church. A little money is collected in a box at the door, and someone from this group makes sure the rent is paid, the building kept neat, and that people are around early on Thursday nights to set up the hundreds of chairs. Someone else sees that there are persons on hand to lead the small teaching and discussion seminars that follow the meetings. One is responsible for preparing, or having another prepare, a short talk on an aspect of Christian living to be given at each meeting. If somebody is in difficulty, these people seek assistance for him. If the meetings appear to be bogging down and getting away from their purpose of worshiping God and promoting spiritual growth, this group tries to discover why and what can be done.

The most obvious manifestation of the charismatic movement is in these communities. All around the country people are becoming more deeply aware of the Holy Spirit and are forming prayer communities to worship God and aid in developing a new style of Christian living. Not all communities are so large (although many are much larger) or so ecumenical. Some are drawn from only one parish or denomination. In a few the people live and relate more closely together; in others they meet only once a week. The form of meeting for prayer is universal: joyful singing, a sense of celebration, a feeling of unity and love, a sharing of new experiences of God's work, prayers of thanksgiving and petition, times for exercising spiritual gifts.

In these communities the essence of the charismatic movement may be seen: that God is at work through the gifts of His Spirit to revitalize His people and form them into communities of love and peace and joy where His name can be praised and

His plan carried out. When I consider what has happened in the last few years, I often think of St. Paul's vision that someday the whole cosmos will be filled with God's presence. There are such groups now in all parts of the country and in almost every denomination. Ten years ago, for example, few Roman Catholics had even heard of the movement; last summer eleven thousand Catholics gathered at Notre Dame University for a national conference on the charismatic renewal. The planning of men could never accomplish such growth or the formation of these prayer meetings and communities. Only the Spirit of God can do it.

The Rebirth of the Church

This account demonstrates several concrete ways in which the charismatic movement is revitalizing Christianity.

1. It is a renewal of faith. That word can mean many things. To some it represents intellectual assent to doctrine. To others, the decision to live one's life in a certain way. In the New Testament it is often used in connection with certain events appearing in the Gospel stories, most often in connection with the experience of Jesus' healing. Both Jesus and Paul speak of increasing and building up one's faith, for they know that there are certain very concrete things which can increase it. This kind of growth in our faith demands that it be closely connected with our experience and not confined to the rather abstract world of intellectual assent or moral duty. Faith, Paul says, is a fruit of the Spirit—which means that it cannot be increased apart from one's experience of the Spirit. This is why the charismatic movement is first of all a renewal of faith; it is a renewal of the work of the Spirit and of those practical experiences that create and increase faith.

We should keep in mind that it was not only the apostles' preaching and teaching but the power of God at work in their midst that drew people to the early Christian assemblies and gave them faith in Jesus Christ. Throughout the book of Acts occur passages like the following:

And great fear came upon every soul for many signs and wonders were done through the apostles and all the believers had all things in common. . . . And with mighty miracles the apostles gave their witness to the resurrection of the Lord Jesus and grace was upon them all and there was not a needy person among them. . . . Through the hands of the apostles many signs and wonders happened among the people and they were all of one mind when they gathered at Solomon's portico and none of the rest of the people dared to join them but the people held them in honor.

These passages indicate that two of the most outstanding things about the early church were the power of God manifest through specific miracles and the strength of their life in community. Throughout Paul's letters he says that it was not only his preaching but also the demonstration of the power of the Spirit that brought faith to his hearers. The charismatic renewal is a rebuilding of faith by reviving these two important aspects of the early assemblies: awareness of the power of God in immediate events and the sense of Christian community.

I have described the ministry of healing through a community. This is a demonstration of the power of the Spirit. Many times I have come to the prayer meetings discouraged about something, and would see person after person who had been freed from narcotic addiction or some physical ailment or even from some form of mental illness that had tormented and perplexed them for years. My faith was revived by this demonstration of the power of the Spirit. Many, many people came to the community who had long ago stopped attending church, because they heard that here the power of God was at work. And they were transformed as every week people stood up and recited the great things the Lord was doing. This is a demonstration of the power of the Spirit that strengthens faith.

It is very hard to believe that God is dead when one sees people healed by His power; it is hard to believe that He is anything other than the way He is pictured in the New Testament—a loving Father. Through the exercise of such spiritual gifts as healing, discernment, and prophecy faith is built up. Many times in the charismatic community I have seen both laymen and ordained persons who were on their way out. They have lost their faith, have become discouraged; God seems absent from their world. Then they come into the community and see God at work. Week after week they see people healed of what seemed to be incurable diseases; they see them freed of burdens they have carried all their lives; they see love growing, peace flourishing, and joy abounding. Soon scripture takes on new meaning, for it becomes not only a narrative of long-past events but an explanation of what they see happening before their eyes.

Another way faith is built up is by sensing the presence of God. Often when people's faith is weak, they simply feel God is absent. A direct sense of His presence counteracts this and is often how nonbelievers come to faith. Once I was at a conference for leaders in the charismatic movement. There were over a thousand people, and when they all began to praise God the sense of His presence was so overwhelming that one could not help but be aware of it. I saw there a photographer who had been sent out from the local paper to cover the story. He was not a believer, had not gone to church for years. But when he came into that assembly and all those people began to sing and pray and praise the Lord, the presence of God was so strong that it overpowered this unbelieving man. No one preached to him or strong-armed him. As soon as he walked in he just felt the presence of the Lord, and fell down on his knees and began to cry. The experience of God created faith in him. And so it is for many: the constant experience of the presence of God builds up their faith.

Moreover, the charismatic movement is a renewal of faith because it revives awareness of the power of God in each person's life. It is startling to see people who were formerly apathetic suddenly begin taking in runaway juveniles or visiting prisons. I have seen nominal church members suddenly start witnessing to the Lord at their jobs and in their neighborhoods. I have seen people who had wrestled with alcoholism for years receive the power to get free. This is a renewal of the power of God in the church and also in each person's life to empower him to do the Lord's work.

2. The charismatic movement is also a renewal of love. There are many ways to think of love—we often think of it as something we *do*. Thus we understand Christianity to mean that we must try to be loving. I am not knocking that, but I do not believe that is what the New Testament means by love. Paul calls love a fruit of the Spirit—not something we do but something the Spirit forms in us, a fruit of the Spirit's work within us. So often when we think of love as something we must do, what we show the world is not love of God but only our strenuous and frustrating efforts to make ourselves more loving. And often we come under condemnation, which is just the opposite of love. We huff and strain and try to be loving, and sooner or later we are bound to fail. Then we begin to condemn and criticize ourselves. Rather than experiencing the love and forgiveness of God which would set us free to love in turn, we come into condemnation and criticism.

This has to do with the complicated theological problem of the relation of law and gospel. The New Testament does not lay the demand on people to make themselves loving; that would be to preach law in place of gospel. Rather it promises that God's Spirit can transform a person and free him to be more loving. When people open up to the Spirit and give it free enough reign in their lives to exercise its gifts, then it begins to flow through them and work in them, and the fruits of the Spirit —love and peace and joy—begin to dwell in them. The charismatic movement renews love because it is a renewal of the Spirit that brings love as its natural fruit.

3. The movement is also a renewal of the church as the body of Christ—i.e., of Christian community. St. Paul is clear that the purpose of the spiritual gifts is to build up the body of Christ: that these endowments belong to the community, and each of us is given such a gift not for himself but for the common good. The gifts of the Spirit and the fruits of the Spirit are corporate. The Christian life is not one of autonomous and isolated individuals; it is a corporate existence, it is life in the Lord's body.

Often I have gone to speak at various churches and people have said, Yes, there was a prayer group here four or five years ago. But Mrs. So-and-So died, or Rev. Such-and-Such left, and the prayer group disappeared. In many areas where there was once a flourishing Pentecostal movement there is now nothing but ashes and a residue of bitterness from spiritual fires that burned too hot because people did not understand that the purpose of the Pentecostal experience was to build up the body of Christ. Now things are different. The Catholic charismatic movement constantly attempts to harness the energy of the movement for forming Christian community. Young people who experience the Spirit are creating communities of the Spirit. Traditional Pentecostals, with a heritage of individualism and animosity toward the church of Rome, are learning from Catholic charismatics the lesson of building up the body of the Lord. Thus is the Spirit drawing all God's people together. Sometimes they move in together; sometimes they form prayer communities like the one I have described where quite diverse members meet regularly in a disciplined way to serve each other and to build up the body of Christ.

This renewal is not only *forming* Christian community but also demonstrating the importance of it. Let me give a personal example. When I became a Christian in college and joined the church, I was told that I would always have ups and downs in my Christian life. And sure enough, I had plenty of them. After I had been in the community in St. Paul for a while I suddenly realized that I was not having ups and downs any more. Not that I was morally perfect or that I felt that Kingdom had fully come; far from it. That has to wait for the end. But I was not having my customary roller-coaster ride from spiritual highs to spiritual valleys and back again. When we left the community and moved to New Jersey, where there was no charismatic community, I suddenly started having ups and downs again. And I realized that this was the Lord teaching me the importance of Christian community. These violent alternations are not inherent in the Christian life; they are the result of trying to live it on one's own. The full Christian life cannot be lived individually but only as a member of the full body of Christ. The Holy Spirit is renewing Christianity by recreating the church as a community.

People often describe charismatic experience *internally,* as it were: how it feels to experience the Spirit. I have not taken that line for two reasons. First, because feelings differ. Some persons have a great emotional rush when they exercise the gifts of the Spirit; some feel nothing at all. It is presumably a matter of temperament, and the Lord respects the kind of people we are. Also some people who have heard this kind of testimony come to doubt their own gifts if they do not have an overwhelming emotional high. That seems wrong to me. Telling whether gifts are really spiritual has little to do with feelings. A religious experience involves the whole person and ought to include all aspects of his or her being, the affections but also the intellect and will. To concentrate too heavily on the emotional side without equal emphasis on the intellect and will falsifies its nature (by making it seem "wholly emotional") and may lead to the traditional Pentecostal tendency to exaggerated emotionalism.

Second, the New Testament never describes the work of the

Holy Spirit in terms of the feelings of the recipients but only in terms of how it manifested itself in concrete renewal. In the charismatic movement almost everyone undergoes powerful and awesome spiritual experiences, but more to the point is the fact that people's faith is built up, the power of God made manifest, love increases, and the church is made into the body of Christ.

Q. Is the charismatic movement predominately among the youth, those under thirty?

A. No. There are charismatic "Jesus-people" among the young, but they are only a small part of the whole movement. Communities I have visited are almost all people in their thirties and forties, although we did have a sizable contingent of young people coming to the meetings in St. Paul. Charismatic meetings are the most diverse church-related meetings I have ever attended. The renewal includes people of all ages who meet together without a generation gap.

Q. Are prayer meetings usually away from the church and during the week?

A. Yes. In St. Paul we rented a church hall but had no connection with the parish itself. Later we had to rent almost a whole parochial school for all the people and activities. The meetings were on Thursday night. There is no official connection with any church, so that people from any church can attend freely.

Q. Does everyone in the group speak in tongues?

A. Yes, almost everyone. I shall say more about tongues later. The importance of this element is always exaggerated by people outside the movement—sometimes by those inside it too. Speaking in tongues is a way into a deeper life in the Spirit, but it is not *synonymous* with that life. It is a way of radically opening yourself to the Spirit so that God can do major things through you. It shows a willing obedience to the Spirit as opposed to the tight rational control we almost always keep as a façade. Most people come into the charismatic experience through speaking in tongues. A friend of mine says, "God doesn't give you the power tools until you have learned to handle the hand tools." Few charismatic people exercise great ministries of healing or prophecy who have not first learned to use tongues. Why that is I'll explain later.

Q. Is speaking in tongues just the result of social pressure?

A. I don't know. This question is often asked. How would one tell? What would be evidence for it being only social pressure? I have been to Pentecostal churches where a great deal of group pressure is put on people, and I have seen neo-Pentecostal meetings where one senses people are being coerced into being prayed for. Obviously I don't approve of either of these practices, nor do they go on in any community of which I have been a member. Sometimes people are just a little hesitant and need some encouragement to cross the threshold and give themselves more to the Lord. I was that way myself. Pastoral encouragement and support is different from coercion. No one should be coerced. It seems rather unlikely that speaking in tongues, which is quite clearly not mere gabbling, *could* be done as a result of mere pressure. Still, how can you tell? Later I shall discuss how to know whether spiritual gifts are really spiritual. That will provide at least one way of discerning whether such "gifts" are the result of social pressure or authentic religious experience.

Of course you assume that if it is the result of social pressure it can't be authentic. Why?

Q. How does participation on Thursday nights affect the relationship of the people involved to their parish life? What happens to them in the more established kinds of worship?

A. I am going to discuss that in great detail at the end. The whole last section is directed to just that question.

Q. It is about eighteen hundred years since the first Pentecost. What has the Spirit been doing in the meantime?

A. Working to build up the body of Christ and carry out the plan of God! Some argue that there has always been a full charismatic movement going on in the church, that there have always been a few who exercised spiritual gifts. Whether that is true or not, I don't really know. I think the Spirit wants to work within the church, but can't work much beyond the level of openness He finds in the people He must work through. The Spirit has always been there, but there hasn't always been the kind of teaching and openness that allows full play of spiritual gifts (I'll be saying more about this, too). There has been openness to the Spirit in other areas, however.

Chapter 2

BIOGRAPHY OF THE SPIRIT

The Birth of the Church

We often say that the day of Pentecost is the birthday of the church. This is not just a piece of pious rhetoric but a fact which must be taken seriously if we are to understand what the church is really all about. There are few reports in the New Testament of great apostolic ministry, many mighty deeds, or inspired preaching until after Pentecost. Rather, Jesus specifically tells the apostles they are not to engage in any activity until they have received the power of the Holy Spirit. (Acts 1:4) It was not until after the day of Pentecost that they burst forth into the world with the full experience of healing and forgiveness and power in their lives. Some clue to the importance of that day may be gleaned from the change that took place in the disciples. Peter, who had denied the Lord, now proclaimed him openly. Disciples who had fled at Jesus' arrest now confronted the authorities face to face. It is the event of Pentecost that accounts for the power of the first Christians—for the confirmed love and forgiveness that filled the early assemblies —for their unshakable sense of community and zeal for the poor.

Another way to see vividly the place of Pentecost in Christianity is to look at the church calendar. The chronology of the church year is also the New Testament chronology of the founding of the church. And I would argue that it is the sequence each one of us passes through in growing as a Christian. As we all know, the year runs from Christmastide to Epiphany to Lent and Passiontide, Good Friday, then Easter, Ascension Day, and finally Pentecost and the Sundays after it. It was this same order of events that the disciples went through, leading up to the founding of the church. Each was important, but none sufficient in itself. Each fulfilled or carried on what went before. Jesus' ministry was not contradicted or negated but fulfilled by his suffering and death. His passion was not put aside but rather fulfilled by his resurrection, and his resurrection by his ascension. And the whole series was further fulfilled on the day of Pentecost. The disciples did not then forget Jesus' ministry, his teaching, his death and resurrection. Yet none of these—or all of them together—were sufficient without the day of Pentecost. Participation in the Pentecostal experience for the disciples and for ourselves does not supersede what has gone before but rather fulfills and completes it.

Many churchgoers, I suspect, only follow their church year part way. All believe in the birth of Jesus and follow his life and ministry as the disciples did. All kneel before the cross on Good Friday and believe he died for us. Hopefully all also come to the empty tomb and, having seen the risen Lord, rejoice in his resurrection. But many, I suspect, stop there. They do not go on to consider the importance of Pentecost. Thus their Christian lives are not fully formed and remain vaguely incomplete and unfulfilled, just as the disciples would have been if they had had only the legacy of the words of Jesus and the events of his life to tell people without the power of his vital presence in their lives. The book of Acts and the letters of Paul make it clear that the early church did not proclaim only the teachings of Jesus or the wonderful events of his life, but actually brought people into a direct experience of his love and power through his communal body, and by the mighty, miraculous works they were able to do. Paul says to the Corinthians, "I did not come to you, brothers, proclaiming the testimony of God in lofty words or wisdom . . . my message was not in seductive words of wisdom but in the demonstration of the Spirit and of miracles."

Let us look, then, at the narrative of the day of Pentecost in Acts 2: how the disciples were all in the upper room when the Spirit came upon them, and there seemed to be flames over their heads, and they began to speak in unknown tongues to those who gathered to hear. People heard the babel of languages, some of which they understood and some of which they did not, and thought the Christians were drunk; just as many today hear about speaking in tongues and assume that those who do it are crazy. But Peter stood up and said that this was the fulfillment of the Old Testament that someday God would pour out His Spirit upon all people.

There are several important things to note about this story.* First—and this is true throughout all of Acts and Paul's letters —when the Spirit comes to people they are always motivated to express it in action. The experience of the Spirit is externalized. In Luke's writings as in Paul, the emphasis is never on the inner feelings of individuals but on ethical and spiritual manifestations. It is never said that people received the Spirit and sat around piously enjoying their warm feelings. Rather they preached, taught, prophesied, spoke in tongues, and took up collections for the poor. What the Lord wants is not a lot of pious prayer groups where everyone wears his soul on his sleeve, which become hothouses of emotionalism in which a lush but exaggerated inner piety develops. What the Lord wants is the building of His body, so that His plan can be carried forth.

*Some years ago I read an article by Roland Allen, the Anglican missionary, entitled "Pentecost and the World," which may be found in his book *The Ministry of the Spirit* (Grand Rapids, Mich.: Eerdmans, 1962). Much of my discussion of Acts 2 is influenced by this essay.

This also means that the New Testament contains no ideas of the Spirit apart from some manifestation. Only through the exercise of gifts of the Spirit and the demonstration of its fruits can the Spirit be recognized. This is the significance of the story in Acts 19 which tells of Paul coming on some disciples and asking them whether they had received the Holy Spirit after they believed in Jesus. They reply that they had been baptized only in the manner of John the Baptist and had never heard of the Spirit. Paul explains to them more about Jesus and then baptizes them in his name and lays hands on them, and they receive the Spirit and begin to speak in new languages and prophesy. Thus Paul finds people whom he recognizes as disciples, yet realizes there is something they have not received. As Fr. Michael Harper, an Anglican priest and leader of the charismatic movement in England, comments, "It is not said that maybe they received the Spirit alone, or privately, or without any manifestations." Paul assumes that when the Spirit comes it comes in a way that is definite and concrete.

The second important thing to note about the story in Acts 2 is that the Spirit is given to everybody, to the common people. In the Old Testament only special individuals—prophets, priests, and kings—were given the Spirit, and then only for short periods of time to enable them to accomplish certain things. For example the Old Testament book of Judges tells of early leaders of Israel, men like Gideon or Samson, who normally went about their business in an ordinary way. When a crisis arose, the Spirit of God is described as coming upon them in some extraordinary way, as when Gideon is said to have defeated a massive army with a few men or Samson is reported as slaying great numbers with a bone for a weapon; but when the crisis passed things would return to normal. The Old Testament describes bands of early prophets called "the sons of the prophets" who wandered around the countryside until the Spirit came upon them and then fell into ecstasy and wild dancing. Amos, a great prophet of the kingdom of Judah, was herding sheep when the Spirit moved him to warn Judah of God's impending judgment. Saul, the first king, was obviously possessed of the Spirit in his early exploits against the Philistine invaders; that is why he was made king. But the Spirit left him in his later days and the crown fell to his enemy David.

These Old Testament figures were not, as traditional Pentecostal theology puts it, "baptized in the Spirit." They received the Spirit only at special times and for specific tasks. The Old Testament also speaks of a future age when God's Spirit will rest upon his people and remain with them. Moses says that he wishes all God's people were prophets, filled with the Spirit. Jeremiah speaks of a time when God will write his new covenant on each person's heart and everyone will know the presence of the Lord. Ezekiel said that the day was coming when God would put his Spirit into his people in a new way. And the prophet Joel foretold an age when God would freely pour his Spirit upon all people, and all would become prophets.

This is what the early church saw happening on the day of Pentecost. All people—common people, young and old, housewives, laborers, officials—everyone was given the Spirit, not just religious officials or prophets, priests, and kings. And they had the Spirit not just for special tasks but for their daily lives as Christians. This elevates the common life of the believer in some sense to the level of the great men of the Old Testament. It means that all Christians are prophets, priests and kings by virtue of sharing in the Spirit. Thus the first letter of Peter tells an ordinary Christian congregation that they are "a chosen race, a royal priesthood, a holy nation, God's own people, in order to declare the wonderful works of him who called you." All Christians, because God's Spirit resides with them, are to carry on the task of the people of the Old Testament—to be God's own people, a spiritual royalty, a congregation of prophets.

The New Testament indicates that in the early Christian assemblies the gift of prophecy worked to encourage and invigorate the church. As I shall discuss below the charismatic movement provides an example of this same phenomenon of prophecy in the present. The coming of the Spirit also makes all Christians priests. Paul says it gives believers the access to God which formerly only the Old Testament priest enjoyed. Through it every Christian has the possibility of a vital ministry of intercessory prayer, previously open only to special figures like Elijah or David. In the charismatic movement men and women experience this priesthood in the Spirit, reviving the worship of their churches. The strengthening of the church through prophecy, the enlivening of prayer, and the revitalizing of worship are all the result of this elevating of the ordinary lives of Christians to possibilities reached by the giants of the Old Testament, by means of the new presence of the Spirit.

A third important aspect of the story of Pentecost in Acts refers to the way in which we think of the apostles. We often imagine them as great men of faith who, by their zeal and commitment, carried out the work of the Lord. This is how they are frequently pictured in Sunday-school material and in sermons. The church uses them as examples, as great heroes of the faith. We call their story the "Acts of the Apostles." But the emphasis in the book of Acts is not on the acts of the apostles but on the action of the Holy Spirit. The book begins with Jesus' promise of this power. The second chapter describes the events on the day of Pentecost, and the rest of the book unwinds from that beginning. It is the freshly fallen Spirit that inspires Peter's sermon to the skeptical onlookers who thought these first Pentecostals crazy. It is the Spirit that inspires the astounding signs the apostles perform. It is a vision inspired by the Spirit that leads Peter to the home of a Roman soldier, and it is the sudden Pentecostal experience of these Romans that opens up for Peter the possibility of spreading the word about Jesus Christ beyond the Jews to the Gentiles. And so on through the rest of the book.

It was not because they were great heroes, nor only because they were disciples or had been with Jesus that they did the amazing things they did. Rather it was primarily because of the Holy Spirit working through them. Thus Peter says to the astonished crowd after he has healed a lame man, "Why are you surprised at this and why do you stare at us as though by our own power or piety we made this man walk?" It was not the personality or even the faith of Peter and John that healed the man, but the Spirit working through them. When we compare our lives with those of the apostles—our feeble church life and lack of faith with *their* overwhelming accomplishments—we make excuses and say, "Well, it's because they were apostles, it's because they had been with Jesus that they accomplished the things they did." The book of Acts makes clear that we cannot fall back on that excuse. It was not primarily because they were apostles; it was not only because they had walked with Jesus; it was not because they were extraordinary human beings, unlike others, but because of the gift of the Spirit that they did the works they did.

Fourth, the book of Acts affects our ordinary view of the apostles in another way. We generally think of them as great preachers and teachers, as indeed they were. But this type of thought often leads us to think that their ministry consisted only in preaching and teaching. Reading the text carefully, one finds that this ministry contained another element as well. For example there is the story in Acts 19, alluded to earlier. Paul finds some disciples who have not received the Holy Spirit, and so instructs them and lays his hands upon them and prays, and they begin to exercise spiritual gifts. Besides being a preacher and a teacher, he was a minister of the Holy Spirit: that is, he not only preached but also passed on the experience of the Spirit to his converts.

As Paul wrote to the Corinthians and as the book of Acts

illustrates time and time again, the apostles were not content with the spoken word; they actually showed forth the presence of the Spirit through the exercise of spiritual gifts and by demonstrating remarkable signs of God's power. They were not content to leave a place having only instructed converts in their faith; they did not go until they had actually passed on to the new churches the experience of the Spirit. The presence of the Spirit, which they had received in a new way on the day of Pentecost, they were able to communicate to others. This was almost always done by the laying on of hands. In the charismatic movement, when people are prayed for to receive the exercise of spiritual gifts (usually with the laying on of hands), a long tradition is being carried on. The apostles' ministry was not only preaching and teaching but also experiencing and expressing the Spirit. They did not expect the lives of their converts to consist only in understanding and activity but also in a living awareness of this power. Their ministry and the life of the church remained incomplete without it.

What was true of the first Pentecostal experience is true of that experience today. As I said before, the word renewal does not mean to create from nothing but to elicit afresh what has been and is still potentially there. Some sectarians assume that the Spirit has left the mainline Christian tradition. To those of us who are in a church tradition this is obviously silly. The Spirit of Christ has never and will never leave his church. Where the Word of Christ is preached and the sacramental life carried on, God continues to be worshiped "in Spirit and in truth" among many who have never heard of the charismatic movement. This is not the point. The movement does not reintroduce the Spirit into the church, but creates a new experience of that Spirit which has been there all along. It allows it to become visibly and tremendously vital in our lives by opening up new channels for God's power.

As the first Pentecost did not replace but rather fulfilled what went before it in the lives of the apostles, so a new Pentecost in our lives (as the late Pope John prayed for it) fulfills the life we have been leading up to this point. As we have seen, that day was the culmination of the ministry and death and resurrection of Jesus; in the same way the Pentecostal experience fulfills and carries forward our baptism, our confirmation, our life of sacrament and service hitherto. The first Pentecost was not something tacked onto the apostles' growth in Christ but an integral part of it. So a new Pentecost is not something appended to our former life to lead us away from church membership, but rather something that should fulfill and renew it and enable us to continue it in a deeper way. Some Pentecostals have been driven from their churches, but those in the present time who say that Pentecostal experience *led* them out of their churches have misunderstood the event. People who suggest that their new experience of the Spirit negates everything that has gone before forget that the first Pentecost fulfilled the work of Christ in the lives of the apostles—did not destroy it.

It should also be clear that what happened to the disciples on the day of Pentecost—their receiving of spiritual gifts—is not an end but a beginning. I have heard some Pentecostals suggest that this experience is the goal of the Christian life. That is not so. The first Pentecost did not mark the close of the apostles' ministry but a new beginning. It was a further initiation, an entrance into a deeper life in the Spirit. Those who imply that people who exercise spiritual gifts are of necessity more mature than those who do not, overlook this fundamental fact. Persons who seek the gifts of the Spirit as an ends in themselves, as though they were a badge of spiritual development or the end of all personal and spiritual problems, are naïve about what the experience really means. It cannot be sought as an end in itself because it *is not* an end in itself, but only the beginning of a deeper life in the Spirit. It is a strengthening and fulfilling of one's life in Christ. It is a reorienting and reempowering of the

Spirit given in baptism, confirmation, and through the sacraments and the Bible. That is why I prefer to call it a release of the Spirit, for that is what spiritual gifts do: they release the power of God present in every Christian for as long as he has been in Christ. Calling it a release, a freeing of the Spirit emphasizes that it must be sought because you want to continue to grow—not because you want (however unconsciously) to stop growing.

Charismatic Movements in the Present

The rediscovery in modern times of these "spiritual gifts" launched the movement known as Pentecostalism—or, as I prefer to call it, the charismatic movement. It seems to have had three different stages, or to have produced three different kinds of groups.* The first I shall call classical Pentecostals, although I am afraid these people who regard themselves as miles removed from the mainline churches, will not like being referred to as "classical" anything. These are your Pentecostal denominations, such as the Assemblies of God, the Church of the Four-Square Gospel, and the various storefront assemblies which seem to spring up like flowers amid the broken concrete of our urban decay.

The movement began at the turn of the century.† In 1900 a Methodist evangelist named Charles Parham opened a Bible school in Topeka, Kansas. There were about forty students. All of them, like the founder of the school, came from the holiness

---

*This distinction between three kinds of groups—classical Pentecostals, neo-Pentecostals, and Catholic charismatics—is common in current discussions of the movement. I gleaned it from the writings of Killian McDonnell, O.S.B.

†Basic histories of the early Pentecostal movement are easily available in Morton T. Kelsey, *Tongue Speaking* (Garden City: Doubleday, 1964); Michael Harper, *As at the Beginning* (Plainfield, N.J.: Logos Press, 1971); John L. Sherrill, *They Speak with Other Tongues* (Westwood, N.J.: Revell, 1964); and John T. Nichol, *Pentecostalism* (New York: Harper & Row, 1966).

movement which grew out of the Methodist Church and emphasized an overwhelming emotional experience of conversion, a literalistic interpretation of the Bible, and the strictest code of personal morality. They came to the school to deepen their faith. Their first assignment, while the principal was out conducting revivals, was to search the New Testament to discover the secret of the power and vitality of the early church. When he returned, everyone was in a state of excitement because they all agreed that the key to the life of the early church had to do with the Holy Spirit. As they prayed together that night they suddenly began to experience unheard-of things. They uttered strange languages, they had an overwhelming urge to speak the word of God, they prayed with effect for healing. Soon they linked up these experiences with what Paul mentioned in Corinthians and came to the conclusion that they were experiencing the same gifts of the Spirit—tongues, healing, prophecy, and so on. Out of this conclusion the Pentecostal movement was born, with its claim that modern man too could receive the same gifts.

They called their experience baptism in the Holy Spirit and began to tell others in the evangelical churches about it. And of course they ran into trouble. It is a dogma in most conservative Protestant churches that human experience of the miraculous or supernatural ended with the apostles. Thus the early Pentecostals were given the cold shoulder. Many were excommunicated from their denominations (just as popular singer Pat Boone was recently expelled from his church for the same reason). Some Pentecostal evangelists were even tarred and feathered as well as beaten by their evangelical brethen. In the first years of the century the Pentecostals made little impact and were hardly noticed in the religious life of America.

Then in 1905 an itinerant Negro Pentecostal evangelist by the name of William Seymour came to Los Angeles to set up his work. Barred from preaching in churches, he rented a storefront. Soon people were experiencing the gifts of the Spirit. Hundreds came. The meeting place grew too small, so they moved to an old abandoned stable. There revival meetings continued for three years. People came from all around the world to see what was going on. Thousands received the baptism in the Spirit and returned home to tell others. From this broken-down building in the slums of Los Angeles, Pentecostal revivals spread to Scandinavia and the British Isles, and from there throughout the world as well as to every major part of the United States. Almost all Pentecostal denominations derived from those meetings in Los Angeles. Throughout the twentieth century the movement grew, until there are now several world-wide denominations as well as churches in almost every country. Both in the United States and throughout the world, the Pentecostals are now the fastest-growing Christian bodies.

Most people, when they think of the charismatic movement, think of classical Pentecostals, and the bad press they have received has colored almost everyone's perception. Such overdrawn images as "Holy Rollers" and "screaming prophets" conjure up pictures of people falling into literal fits of salvation, with loss of all control and maybe even some element of religious fraud. It is important to remember that all the leaders and almost all early converts to Pentecostalism were from the conservative evangelical tradition. They had only a fundamentalist framework by which to interpret their experience. Like most evangelical Americans, they were emotional, moralistic, and anti-intellectual. They could only explain what happened to them in terms they knew, and so they saw it in a highly individualistic, emotional way, carrying over much of the cultural ethos of fundamentalist Protestantism. This is not to criticize, for they understood the experience in the only way they could, given their background. The problem arises because they, and even more sophisticated interpreters of the movement, have been unable for the most part to separate the Pentecostal event itself from the interpretation they gave it. Even today, most people assume that to be a Pentecostal is to be a fundamentalist —a literalist in scriptural exegesis and an emotional fanatic in piety—for it is difficult to distinguish the essential experience from the wrappings in which classical Pentecostals have packaged it.   **1783508**

Evangelical pietism, out of which the Pentecostals sprang, tended to see life as a series of dramatic experiences, the first of which was conversion through a crisis of sin and salvation which overturned one's previous existence. The holiness movement added to this another experience called a "second blessing," which assured one's personal holiness. Then the early Pentecostals took over the scheme and added a final step, baptism in the Holy Spirit. Each group argued that the Christian life was not complete until their particular stage had been achieved: the evangelicals said one had to pass through a crisis conversion; the holiness people said one's life was not complete without a second blessing; the classical Pentecostals insisted that one be baptized in the Spirit. According to this, one might be baptized, converted, sound in doctrine, and upright in life and yet not a full Christian if one did not exercise gifts of the Spirit.

This rather special understanding is not inherent in the charismatic experience itself; it was merely part of the culture and theology which the early Pentecostals took from their evangelical ethos. It made sense of their lives, but for many people (myself included) it has several drawbacks. For it fragments— or segments—the life of the Christian. There is an organic connection between the exercise of spiritual gifts and the whole of Christian life; thus they should not be set over against baptism or conversion. Early Pentecostal theology focuses too heavily on the individual's emotional experience by understanding baptism in the Spirit by an analogy with the pietistic view of conversion: i.e., as a religious crisis. The resulting emotionalism and individualism account for many of the ensuing problems. More-over, early Pentecostal theology carried a harsh judgment on those who are not charismatic. I would agree that the Lord wants everyone to exercise spiritual gifts so that His church may be built up and His plan carried out, but this does not mean that those who do not are sub-Christian—only that the Lord has more in store for them then they are presently aware of.

This brings me to the second group I want to mention, whom I shall call neo-Pentecostals, for they are those in the mainline Protestant churches who have had the Pentecostal experience but have remained in their denominations.* During the fifties and sixties the Pentecostal movement moved out of its ob-scurity into the popular press. This was due to two factors. One was the ministry of David Du Plessis, minister of the Pentecos-tal church in South Africa. In 1936 he was confronted by a member of his church who laid on him the following words: "You have been in Jerusalem long enough. . . . I will send you to the uttermost parts of the earth . . . you will bring the message of Pentecost to all churches. . . . God is going to revive the churches in the last days and through them turn the world upside down. . . ."† Pentecostals had grown up in awareness of the hatred and suspicion they generated among other churches. Now this young minister was told that he must go to all these churches that had despised the movement, for God was going to renew them all, Protestant and Catholic alike, in a revival that would make the Pentecostal movement itself seem like nothing. It is startling to read this prophecy now, in light of all that has happened. Three weeks later Du Plessis received an invitation to come to the United States, and since then he has become one of the most widely journeyed Christian leaders in

---

*For examples of this group see Harper, op. cit.; Kelsey, op. cit.; and Sherrill, op. cit.

†Quoted in Harper, op. cit., p. 51. For Du Plessis's own story see his book *The Spirit Bade Me Go* (Dallas: published by the author, 1961).

the world. In the fifties he visited the World Council of Churches, then attended in Germany the first ecumenical conference sponsored by the WCC, then was invited to the second assembly in Evanston, Illinois, as a member of the staff. He was a visitor at Vatican II. Since then he has spoken to representatives of Christian groups throughout the world and given them a new openness to the Pentecostal movement.

The other development during the fifties and sixties was that groups from the various mainline Protestant churches, both clergy and lay, began meeting together to study the scriptures and deepen their spiritual life. The same things began to occur among them as had happened to those early Pentecostals in Topeka, Kansas, such as speaking in strange tongues, and praying with new power for the healing of the sick. Few of these groups knew of each others' existence, and few outside them knew what was going on. But all this changed on Passion Sunday of 1960, when the rector of the Episcopal church in Van Nuys, California, got up to preach. Fr. Bennett had heard of the Pentecostal experience from a neighboring Episcopal priest, who had heard of it at a prayer meeting at the home of two of his most loyal and faithful parishioners. Fr. Bennett then attended these meetings and had the same experience. In the following year many of his parishioners, including wardens and vestry, became involved. It was kept hush-hush for almost a year, but rumors began to spread, including false allegations that members were rolling on the floor and engaging in other grotesque and ecstatic if not immoral practices. Finally, on Passion Sunday, Fr. Bennett told the whole story to his congregation. The cat was out of the bag, and the dissension was there for all to see. One of the curates removed his vestments and stormed out of the church. The treasurer suggested that Fr. Bennett resign, which he did. The bishop of his diocese issued a pastoral letter banning any Pentecostal activity in the diocese; the other bishop in California, the late James Pike, followed suit and condemned the Pentecostals, forbidding such prayer meetings in the churches.

Soon it hit the press, and other involved Episcopal priests as well as charismatic ministers from most Protestant denominations were exposed to publicity and often to harassment from their church superiors. As the existence of these groups was brought to light, churches went into dissension over what to do about them. Often the recent Pentecostal converts were arrogant and self-righteous, their zeal outstripping their wisdom as they were forced to defend themselves. Often those not involved reacted defensively and refused to consider the issue in an open and objective manner. Thus the movement got off to a poor start in many denominations. Nevertheless, it has spread throughout the mainline denominations, until now there is probably no major Christian group in America without some charismatic activity. The Presbyterians have formed a national organization of Pentecostal Presbyterians, and the Presbyterian church has issued a generally favorable report on the movement. Last summer the Lutherans held a national conference on the charismatic movement in the Lutheran church.

Two points should be kept in mind when considering the neo-Pentecostal movement. First, in its early stages it received a lot of publicity, and this was probably detrimental. It made the participants very self-conscious, and when people are self-conscious they often become defensive and are either unduly aggressive or withdraw into themselves. The "clique-ish" mentality of some early neo-Pentecostals came from the sudden pressure of publicity upon them, forcing them to band together to ward off the glare of the media and the accusations of their fellow church members. Persons who themselves were very new to the experience and had not had time to absorb and reflect on it or come to maturity in it were forced to defend it to the public eye and often to their ecclesiastic superiors. Immaturity and defensiveness do not provide the best atmosphere in which to evaluate a movement. The scars of this awkward beginning may still be seen, and to this day some of these groups retain an atmosphere of suspicion and defensiveness.

Second, many neo-Pentecostals came into the movement with very little knowledge of what it was about. It was often customary for people to be "prayed with" to receive the exercise of spiritual gifts with little prior instruction and no follow-up. On their own with a very powerful and poorly understood experience in their lives, it is a miracle that more of them did not go off and get into trouble. More important—and this is a real word of criticism against the mainline churches—there was so little teaching to be had and so few theological resources in their own traditions to help them deal with this area of experience that they turned increasingly to the classical Pentecostals for instruction. There is nothing inherently wrong with this, since we all have much to learn from each other. But more and more, the new groups took on the interpretations, attitudes, and style of the early fundamentalist Pentecostals. This forced many of them out of the mainstream of their own church traditions. Often they became very emotional and anti-intellectual, very literal in their use of scripture and rigidly moralistic in their ethical teaching. This is true even of those who came from churches with a quite different approach to scripture and with long traditions of theological understanding. I have met several Episcopal priests involved in the neo-Pentecostal movement whose doctrine and style are indistinguishable from those of ministers I know in the Assemblies of God. In some cases the classical Pentecostals have even been the more sober and reflective and conscious of tradition. Thus the new groups—spiritually separated from their own churches—were often rightly the subject of suspicion on the part of remaining church members and the movement did not influence the theological or liturgical life of the churches as a whole.

The third and final group to be mentioned in the charismatic or Pentecostal movement is that in the Roman Catholic church.* Again, this began quite unexpectedly. A group of Catholic students from Duquesne University were on a retreat to deepen their spiritual lives. As they prayed together, strange and unforeseen things began to happen. Let me quote from one report.

This "Duquesne weekend" as it has come to be called was certainly one of the most remarkable incidents in the story of the Pentecostal movement. . . . All day Saturday the group met for prayer and study. Saturday evening had been set aside for relaxation . . . as one girl put it "we were tired of praying and we weren't going to spend the evening in prayer too." . . . One of the girls, a Duquesne coed . . . had felt drawn to the chapel, and there had felt the almost tangible presence of the Spirit of Christ. In awe she left the chapel and quickly urged others in the building to join her there. By ones and twos the small group made their way to the chapel. And as they were gathering together there in prayer, the Holy Spirit poured himself out upon them. There was no urging, there was no direction as to what had to be done. The individuals simply encountered the person of the Holy Spirit as others had several weeks before. Some praised God in new language, some quietly wept for joy, others prayed and sang. They prayed from ten in the evening until five in the morning.†

From Duquesne the report of this experience was carried to Notre Dame University, where a large charismatic group was established. Some young men from the Notre Dame group went to Ann Arbor, Michigan, where there is now a charismatic community of almost a thousand members. These Roman Catholics were utterly amazed at what was happening, since they had never heard of anything like it before; yet they were also

*The best history of this group is Kevin and Dorothy Ranaghan, *Catholic Pentecostals* (New York: Paulist Press, 1969). See also their *As the Spirit Leads Us* (New York: Paulist Press, 1971); and Edward O'Connor, *The Pentecostal Movement in the Catholic Church* (Notre Dame, Ind.: Ave Maria Press, 1971).
†Ranaghan and Ranaghan, op. cit., pp. 21–22.

very open to the leading of the Spirit, and from Notre Dame and Ann Arbor the movement has spread until there are now Catholic charismatic communities of several hundred people each in all the major cities of the Middle West, as well as many along the east and west coasts. American Roman Catholic bishops have recently issued a statement in support of the movement; several bishops are involved, and a large national organization has been set up.

There are some important things to be said about this phase of the movement. First, these Roman Catholics were obviously not fundamentalists and did not interpret their experience in categories drawn from evangelical Protestantism. The new events thus did not lead to the problems of overemotionalism and anti-intellectualism associated with classical Pentecostals. Second, they had a strong sense of the history of the church and its theology, and therefore of the corporate nature of the Christian life. This kept the Catholic Pentecostals from the exaggerated individualism of many of the other two types of groups. Rather, they interpreted the experience in ways much closer to St. Paul: as being for the building up of the body of Christ and its work of service. This strong sense of the church also kept the Catholic Pentecostals from any sectarian tendencies. They saw quite rightly that the goal of the movement was to renew the church, not to set up new churches.

This orientation toward the church, which has kept the Catholic charismatic movement safely away from sectarianism and sound in its theology, may also give it some problems. In many of the communities I have visited I have begun to notice a preoccupation with the same issues of authority and discipline that characterize the church of Rome generally. Often discussions in these communities focus on the problems of leadership and lines of authority within them. In contrast to the anarchy of much of classical Pentecostalism and the romantic utopian outlook of many previous American experiments with religious community, the Catholic recognition that there must be authority, structure, and discipline within community is a necessary balance. Some Catholics seem to feel instinctively that in any religious organization there must be a hierarchy in which certain ones have authority over the rest. Scripture makes clear that some pastoral authority within the body of Christ is inspired by the Spirit and necessary to the building up of the church, but this strong proclivity for organization may have preserved certain Catholic communities from the chaos of other forms of Pentecostalism only to lead them to the opposite extreme of more organization and authority than is necessary for the work of the Lord.

This brief historical sketch has been designed to pinpoint several important issues. First, that the charismatic movement arose spontaneously. It was always unexpected. Classical Pentecostals came into being when groups of evangelical Protestants were meeting together to deepen their spiritual lives. The neo-Pentecostals appeared, not through proselytizing efforts on the part of the classical pentecostals (most of whom felt that the mainline churches were on their way to hell), but when groups of Protestants met together to deepen *their* spiritual life. The movement arose in the Catholic sphere, not through missionary activity on the part of other churches, but when groups of Catholics prayed together to deepen their spiritual life. Each group was born indigenously within its own tradition. Becoming involved in the charismatic movement did not (and does not) mean leaving one's own church and joining a classical Pentecostal outfit. The movement is not the result of one group's forcing itself upon others; it is simply something that may happen whenever Christians meet together to deepen their spiritual life and are totally open to the leading of the Spirit.

Second, this history shows that one can (and must) distinguish the Pentecostal experience itself from the way it is interpreted. When it arose within an evangelical Protestant setting it was

interpreted in terms of evangelical thought. But it is not necessary to see it in that light. Like any basic Christian experience
(such as salvation, sanctification, or the sacramental life), it is
amenable to a variety of perspectives depending on one's prior
theological commitments. It neither proves nor disproves anyone's theology. Hopefully there can be a balance in this (and all)
genuine religious experience between the experience itself and
the framework in which it is interpreted. None of the participants in the charismatic movement have been so open as to
allow the Spirit to purge them totally of what is unnecessary in
their own traditions. As time goes on and the Spirit is given free
reign to work, it is drawing many of these diverse groups together by purging them of their cultural accretions. The almost
automatic but mistaken identification of the movement solely
with the classical Pentecostals still leads many to criticize it as
necessarily involving extreme emotionalism, individualism, and
anti-intellectualism. Many who are attracted to much that goes
on in the movement are afraid to be drawn in for fear they will
have to give up their own tradition and adopt a quite alien style
and theology. It is extremely important to make clear that the
Pentecostal experience is something distinct from the perspective given it by the classical Pentecostals, and amenable to
sound interpretation within Anglican, Roman Catholic, Reformed, and Lutheran theology.

Thirdly, this brief history shows that the charismatic movement need not lead to sectarianism. It often appears to do so.
All the earliest Pentecostals came out from their churches and
started new sects. Some of the early neo-Pentecostals created
dissension and schism in their churches over the exercise of
spiritual gifts—particularly "tongues." I think careful examina-
tion of the facts will show something my own experience bears
out 100 percent: namely, that in this movement sectarianism
results only from within an already existing, strongly sectarian
tradition.

Once while I was talking to a group of Protestants and Catholics, the wife of a Methodist minister persisted in giving me a hard time—asking very hostile questions and interrupting with snide comments. It turned out that her husband's church had been disrupted by members who had come into the charismatic movement. When I had taken all I could, I finally said to her that although I was not a Methodist I suspected I knew how their Sunday-school material taught church history. It probably said that when the church of Rome got too corrupt, the church of England broke off from it, and then, when the church of England fell into ruins, Wesley had to leave it in order to gather a true spiritual fellowship. None of this is historically true, but it is the American sectarian version of English church history. And so, I said, you can't fill people with sectarian teaching and not expect them to act on it. The arguments these Pentecostals had used against her husband were the same as her Methodist ancestors used against the Anglican church. And they had learned them as good, pious Methodists!

The point is that in traditions like the Anglican, Roman Catholic, and Lutheran, where sectarianism is not a part of the heritage, the charismatic movement need not lead to sectarianism. It is only where stress is laid on a sectarian view of the church and its history (which is to say, in most churches in this country, since sectarianism set the predominate tone for the American scene) that the charismatic movement is naturally seen in a sectarian perspective. Among Catholic and Lutheran Pentecostals whom I know, the experience is interpreted, on the contrary, as having for its purpose the renewal of that whole church—not a separation from it. Catholic charismatic leaders continually stress that the goal of the movement is the renewal of the church, and in the context of that kind of teaching—along with those fruits of the Spirit called love and patience—there is no danger of sectarianism.

Q. I get annoyed when I hear neo-Pentecostals speak of themselves as Christians with the strong implication that those
who aren't Pentecostal aren't Christian. Do you feel this is
characteristic of the movement?

A. Sometimes I *feel* that it is. But this is really a sociological
question which I don't have the hard data to answer. We
have all met people who give us this impression. I must say
in strict honesty that, when I speak in various places on the
charismatic movement, I often have to spend most of my
time and energy simply undoing what well-meaning but
overzealous Pentecostal types have done by not "making
love their aim," as St. Paul says. Most of my work involves
trying to "turn back on" people who have been turned off
by exactly what you mention. The burden of what I want to
say here is to counteract precisely that attitude.

Chapter 3

THE GIFTS OF THE SPIRIT

Understanding Spiritual Gifts

Paul tells the Corinthians, "Brothers, I do not want you to be uninformed about spiritual gifts" (1 Cor. 12). What would he say today? The present church is not merely uninformed about spiritual gifts; rather there seems to be a determined, invincible ignorance of them. Most people are simply not interested. Some are actually afraid of them.

What are these gifts? Paul says "each one is given a manifestation of the Spirit for the common good." This tells us three things about them right away. (1) They are gifts intended to be direct channels for the Spirit of God. They are not ordinary human endowments. The gift of teaching is not what an education major acquires in school, nor is that of tongues what one would gain through a Berlitz course. The gift of healing is not what a physician has after medical training. These traits are not part of ordinary human nature or gained by natural effort. They are supranatural gifts from God for His purpose in the world. And they must be used according to His will or they will backfire. (2) Since they are from the Spirit, they are signs of the Spirit. Paul calls them manifestations of the Spirit; that is, they actually manifest—display—the presence and power of God. (3) They are given for the common good. The purpose of spiritual gifts is to build community. They are not intended to make one person holier than another or to earn merit in the sight of God, but to transform Christians into the kind of people who can live in community, each having a role in which he can serve his brothers and sisters. Thus Paul speaks of the gifts as a "service," a ministry. This is true in two ways. Exercise of such gifts is a service to the church, for through them it is guided and strengthened and built up. They are also a service to the world, for thus God's plan for His creation is carried forth. Spiritual gifts are tools, they are the equipment the Lord supplies to His people to do His work.

How do these general remarks fit in with the specific gifts? Let us look at those enumerated in Paul's letter to the Corinthians. I should like to divide this list into three categories.* First, teaching gifts, those of "wisdom" and "knowledge." We must keep in mind what I have said above: that these are not ordinary human endowments but channels of operation of God's Spirit. When you hear a lecture by a naturally good teacher, you come away impressed by the erudition and articulateness of the speaker. Human learning, quite reasonably, calls attention to the achievements and eloquence of the teacher. Spiritual teaching shows forth not the erudition of the teacher but rather the presence of God; it does not draw attention to the teacher but the Spirit. Human teaching excites the mind and fills the head with new data. Spiritual teaching goes beyond this, for in it the Holy Spirit effects an experience of what is being taught. Through such teaching one not only learns *about* spiritual truth, but becomes actually and directly aware of it.

Let me give some examples of what I mean. I was once involved in a workshop on growing in the Spirit during one of the national conferences of the Catholic charismatic movement. It was a whole day of teaching and praying together. In

*For these categories I am indebted to Stephen Clark's *Spiritual Gifts* (Pecos, Texas: Dove Publications).

the course of the day people not only learned about growth in the Spirit; they actually *grew* in the Spirit. It was phenomenal to see the changes that took place in them in one short day. I remember a young girl who had just come into Christianity after a long stint as a witch and a drug addict. She still bore the scars of her background and was prone to be disruptive. The leaders of the conference prayed about her, and part of the schedule was a talk on the love of God. During it she experienced that love embracing her and was set free from whatever made it necessary for her to interrupt people.

I remember once hearing a sermon on the forgiveness of God. As it went on, I felt that forgiveness washing over me. On another occasion, at a talk on the spiritual life, I looked around and could sense both in myself and on the faces around me that the whole assembly was being filled with the Spirit as the man spoke. These are random examples of the teaching gifts of the Spirit, working not only to instruct but to bring people into an experience of God's presence.

The second category I shall call sign gifts, "faith, healing, miracles." These gifts too are for building up the church and carrying out God's work and nothing builds up the faith of a community like seeing the power of God in action. This was brought home to me at the same workshop on growth in the Spirit. In the course of the day there were several remarkable healings, although we were not speaking of healing at all. Witnessing the power of God in these signs did more than anything we said to build up people who were new in the Spirit. Sometimes I have gone to community meetings when my faith was faltering, and would hear all the witness of what the Lord had done in other people's lives that week and feel myself being built up and restored. What attracted people to the early church and often attracts people to charismatic assemblies today is this demonstration and witness of the power of the Spirit. Some may come seeking only signs and wonders and refuse to be humbled before the Lord. But many others are made humble and awestruck when they see the power of God at work, and these become more deeply committed and more supple to His will.

Signs and miracles not only build up the faith of the body of Christ, but also carry out the plan of God for the world. His purpose for His creation is a function of His love and concern, which healing and miracles also demonstrate. They give us a foretaste of that time when the divine plan will be complete; there will be no more illness or disharmony, and every work will praise the Lord. "Signs" demonstrate even in the present moment that God loves and cares for and dwells with His people.

The third category is the most controversial—that of revelational gifts of prophecy, discernment, and tongues and their interpretation. "Prophecy" means many things to many people. For some it is synonymous with preaching. For others it refers to a particularly critical application of the gospel to the social-political problems of the day. For still others it means the ability to foretell the future. All of these may be true in some sense, but I think it is clear that Paul is referring to something quite different. Prophecy, like all the spiritual gifts, is primarily for building up or renewing the church. It manifests the presence of God. Thus Paul seems to mean speaking a special word to the assembly. This word comes from the Lord and has little to do with a human gift for homiletics or unraveling the complexities of the current political scene or a psychic talent for foretelling the future. Paul says the prophet "builds up, encourages, and consoles men . . . the one who prophesies builds up the church." Much of what passes for prophecy these days tears down the church and frightens its members rather than "consoling" them. This is not because it is judmental; spiritual prophecy may be as judgmental as the gospel. But judgment is never, in the gospel, an end in itself. The Holy Spirit judges in order to heal; God condemns only to restore. Modern-day "prophecy" is often negative and destructive because men do not perceive it as coming from the Lord. It seems based more on human ingenuity than on the Holy Spirit's presence.

Spiritual prophecy, then, is speaking a word from the Lord to his body (either a large assembly or a single member of that body). It is not just speaking what comes into one's mind as though that were the word of God. The word of the Lord, Jeremiah says, is like a hammer and a fire, and generally before a person gives a prophecy to a meeting he will feel an "anointing," a pulsing of the Spirit filling him to give the message. As with all gifts of the Spirit, the community must discern whether it is a genuine word from the Lord. After a true prophecy is given, one becomes aware of a sense of enlightenment and joy spreading through the meeting. Paul does not recommend credulity or blind faith in supposed prophets. Rather he says that while a prophet is speaking the rest must judge carefully what is said [1 Cor. 14:29].

He also says that prophecy is the most important gift for building up the church, and this is clearly so. Many times I have seen prayer groups struggling along, and it is not until the gift of prophecy is exercised and the Lord speaks directly to His people that they begin to form into true community. In a charismatic assembly I once attended we began with mostly intercessory prayer, and the time of waiting on the Lord to speak in prophecy was very brief. Later the time of prophecy grew to half the meeting. It was the time most of us looked forward to, for it was when the Lord directly taught and guided us. After that period almost everyone reported being renewed, revived, and lifted up. At first the prophecies were generally words of encouragement and hope, for we were a struggling little community. Later they began showing us areas where we needed to deepen our commitment. Occasionally they showed us what the Lord was about to do and why we must work on a specific area of our Christian lives. Always when we concentrated on these areas remarkable things happened in the life of the community. Thus we were taught of the Lord. No wonder Paul encourages the Corinthians to prophesy, "so that all may be taught and all may be encouraged."

There is some ambiguity about what the gift of discernment refers to. Generally I take it to mean having the Holy Spirit reveal something to you that you do not naturally know. I remember once someone coming to me after a meeting and asking if I would pray with her for a bad infection. I did not know her at all. As we prayed for healing, I could "sense" some things about her life. So I stopped praying and asked her about them. She was dumfounded, but it turned out that she was living with a very disordered family, hated being there, and could not resign herself to it. So we prayed about that, and her infection cleared up by the time she left the meeting.

I once met some people from a charismatic community I was going to visit. It was clear even to them that they had serious problems, but not exactly what they were. Even before I arrived or they had said very much, it was apparent to me that the difficulties revolved around one or two persons in the community. On the basis of what we discussed, they were able to tackle and overcome these problems.

Someone came to our own community who seemed very distressed. One of the other members came up to me after the meeting and asked if I thought we should pray for that person. It certainly seemed like a good idea, and so we asked the person concerned if we could pray with him. The answer was a defensive and definite No. I never believe one should pressure anyone into prayer, so turned away, but my friend really had the Spirit of the Lord and said, "Jim and I will pray for you, and if you want to join us you can." So we went into a room to pray, and sure enough, the newcomer came along and knelt down beside us. I did not know what to say, and so made a kind of lame prayer for general healing. Then the other member of the community started to pray, and in praying laid out before the Lord many troubled areas in the life of this person with whom we had never spoken before. Needless to say, he was overwhelmed, but he was also healed of these disturbing elements in his life. These are examples of the gift of discernment.

Probably most controversial is the gift of tongues. It receives the most publicity and is the most common gift in the charismatic movement; yet it is no doubt the least important, although nothing God does can be called unimportant. There are many questions as to what it means in scripture and in the present-day renewal. The New Testament seems to have in mind real languages other than those of the speakers. The New English Bible translates the word glossalalia as "ecstatic utterance," but that is an interpretation rather than a translation, for the Greek word simply means language and there is no evidence that "tongues" need be any more ecstatic than speaking English. Some linguistic study of glossalalia has been done, but the results seem (to me) very inconclusive. Speaking in tongues as I have heard it sounds just like people speaking a sonorous foreign language you don't understand. I know someone who, when lecturing on the charismatic movement, always plays a taped example of speaking in tongues. Since I feel that the gifts of the Spirit are not for public display but belong in the context of the Christian assembly, I cannot agree with this practice. But it does make a point. People are usually astonished when they hear it, for they expect something like nonsense gibberish or baby talk, where as in fact it sounds like a foreign language radio station. I have known people to visit a community when there has been a good deal of glossalalia, and ask afterward why no one spoke in tongues. They were expecting something wild and irrational and so did not recognize it when they heard it—they assumed someone *was* in fact speaking in a foreign language.

There is probably no way to settle the theoretical question of the nature of the gift. Paul clearly thought of "tongues" as real languages, and there seem to be cases in the present of people speaking a recognizable language they could not have learned naturally, which give some credence to this view.

Most people who come into the charismatic movement find this the easiest gift to yield to. It has the immediate effect of revitalizing the individual by releasing the flow of the Spirit into his life. Its effects are not primarily cognitive. Thus the question of whether or not "tongues" are real languages is only tangentially relevant; the gift is not usually used cognitively to edify the mind (that would be wisdom or teaching). Usually it renews the individual by allowing the Holy Spirit a freer reign in his life. As the Spirit is released and openly allowed to be manifest through them, people find it easier to yield themselves to higher gifts like prophecy or discernment.

Like all the gifts of the Spirit, this one, too, is for building up the church and showing the presence of God. Wherever the Spirit is allowed to operate freely His presence becomes more real. Thus if a person consistently prays in tongues and opens himself more to the Spirit of God, he will gradually be renewed. The same is true of a large assembly. When a whole assembly gives free reign to the Spirit by praying in tongues, the presence of God is realized in a more potent way. In the community I belonged to in Minnesota, when there were six or seven hundred people singing in tongues and praying in the Spirit, the divine presence was unmistakable, with such a powerful sense of it that skeptics, unbelievers, and even reporters who had come out of curiosity were overwhelmed by it and often joined the community. Christ's church and his people are recreated by a sense of his presence, and his presence is increased by a free flow of his spirit. Thus individuals and communities are renewed by praying in tongues.

We can now begin to answer the question: What are the spiritual gifts for? First of all, they are to invigorate the church and its members by manifesting the power of God and allowing the body to be easily led by its Head. When one's faith is weak, one can see the mighty signs the Lord has done. When one feels that God is far away, one can experience the leading of the Lord through the gifts of discernment. A fuller sense of the presence and power of God automatically builds the faith of the church and its members. We live in a skeptical, "God-Is-Dead" sort of an age; the gifts of the Spirit demonstrate that, on the contrary, God is alive and at work among His people.

Second, spiritual gifts equip the body of Christ for its work. The church is Christ's body in the world; he has no other. The Spirit in order to work in the physical world must work through people. This is why Paul says that we should earnestly desire the spiritual gifts. It makes a lot of sense once we understand that such gifts are part of God's own equipment for building up the church and carrying out His work in the world. They are important to have. In these days, when according to the media the church is steadily losing ground and much of it seems to lack vitality and support, God's own power is desperately needed.

I spent some time last summer refurbishing an old house we had just bought. My father came up to give us a hand and brought a large power saw. It would not make sense for me to refuse to use it. In writing a book, it would not make sense for me to refuse to use a typewriter. These are tools I need to be effective. In the same way, the spiritual gifts are in their own way tools our heavenly Father provides us with. They are instruments we need in order to be effective. If the secularist trend of the times continues, it will become harder and harder for Christians to refuse to use them.

Two Popular Responses

The phenomenal growth of the charismatic movement has generated two popular lines of criticism: one theological and the other psychological. Much of the theological rejection of early Pentecostalism on the part of Protestant groups derives from the classic insistence of Reformed theology that the age of miracles ended with the apostles. Any claim to supernatural works was automatically regarded as spurious. The Reformation was born in the heat of controversy with the church of Rome, which validated its position as the true church by pointing to the miracles done in its midst. To counter this, John Calvin argued that the miraculous gifts were bestowed on the church as (1) a support to the preaching of the word, and (2) a help to the church when it was young and weak. After the death of the apostles they were no longer needed, and so God withdrew them. What remained was the primary focus of the early church: the preaching of the word. Thus Calvin writes "The gift of healing, like the rest of the miracles, which the Lord willed to be brought forth for a time, has vanished away in order to make the new preaching of the Gospel marvelous forever."* Therefore, he reasons, the Roman validation of its claims by miracles is false.

This line of argument was strengthened in nineteenth-century American Protestantism by a movement called dispensationalism, which divided history into a series of "dispensations" —periods of time in which God did certain things to prepare for the next stage, but which were proper only to the moment. Thus, under the Old Testament dispensation God instituted the Jewish sacrificial system as a type of Christ's sacrifice. With the coming of the new covenant, these forms of the old dispensation passed away. This theology was mainly designed to help believers calculate when Christ would come again, but it gave added impetus to the idea that certain gifts belonged solely to the apostolic dispensation. Many early Pentecostals were run

*The Institutes of the Christian Religion, trans. F. L. Battles (Philadelphia: Westminster Press, 1960), p. 1467.

out of their churches because of this line of theological reasoning, which still accounts for the animosity toward the charismatic movement in some evangelical quarters.

The argument of Reformed theology that the charismatic movement is a spurious spirituality has two parts: the subordination of the apostles' miracles to their preaching, and the cessation of such miracles after their death. We have already seen that the New Testament will not support the first contention; it often emphasizes that it was the power of God manifest in the church that drew people to it, and Paul says that his ministry frequently consisted in the demonstration of the power of the Spirit. The second contention too is simply unfounded. The gifts of the Spirit did not end with the apostles. Justin Martyr, writing in the middle of the second century, said, "It is still possible to see among us women and men who possess the gifts of the Spirit of God." Irenaeus, a contemporary of Justin, describes many spiritual gifts at work in the church of his day, including healing, prophecy, discernment, and the power to raise the dead. Tertullian, who wrote at the beginning of the third century, speaks of witnessing the gifts of the Spirit in the church. During this time the first new Pentecostal movement, the Montanists, arose. Like many of their successors, they fell into fanaticism sectarianism and heresy, but the fact that numerous strongholds of early Christianity (in Asia Minor, Gaul, North Africa) were sympathetic to Montanism indicates that the appeal to the Spirit was far from dead in the third century. And they left their mark on the church: the great theologian, Tertullian joined them late in his life, and one of the most revered martyrs of the early church, Perpetua, was a Montanist. Two centuries later, Augustine indicates that the gifts of the Spirit could still occasionally be seen in the church. Thus the argument that the *charismata* ended with the apostolic age is simply untrue.

In keeping with modern culture, probably the most prevalent frame of reference for interpreting Pentecostalism is that of psychology. This has so far proven nothing at all about the charismatic experience except the mental health of those who have it. But the repeated appeal to this criterion reveals our society's tacit assumptions as to the wide-ranging validity and value of the social sciences and psychology in particular. Most of the mainline church reports on the movement have relied heavily upon social-scientific studies; when Bishop Pike forbade the practice he linked it to schizophrenia. And almost all attacks I have seen (whether by conservative Protestants, nonbelieving students of religious phenomena, or the popular imagination) somewhere contain the insinuation that charismatics are just plain crazy. I am under no illusion that any evidence will unseat so deeply ingrained a prejudice as the idea that speaking in tongues is a form of mental illness, but we must consider what is known of the matter anyway.

The most comprehensive report I know of to date which is relatively accessible is the 1967 Report of the Pentecostal Movement Research Committee of the Department of Anthropology of the University of Minnesota. Its results are cited in two articles in the *Journal for the Scientific Study of Religion:* one in 1968 (VII/1) by Virginia Hine and Luther Gerlach entitled "Pentecostals' Growth" (pp. 23–40) and the other in 1969 (VIII/2) by Virginia Hine entitled "Glossolalia" (pp. 211–26). The investigators found no indication of any relation between Pentecostalism and any type of personality disorder. In many cases they found the Pentecostals had a greater degree of emotional health (whatever that may be) than the population at large. All major modern studies of this phenomenon bear out these conclusions. There seems to be some animus rooted in the social-scientific psyche which cannot accept these findings, and so study after study is done, always with the same results.

Anton Boisen, an early pioneer in the psychology of religion, worked with the Holy Rollers. He found no special incidence of mental illness among them. He also cites several case histories of individuals he treated in a mental hospital who later had charismatic experience and always found it therapeutic and beneficial to their mental health (*Psychiatry* 2 [1939], 204–13). Alexander Alland reports in a study of black Pentecostals that he found them well-adjusted and normal psychologically, with no evidence of schizophrenia or hysteria (*J.S.S.R.*, cited above, I/2 [1961], 204–13).

Ari Kiev, in the book *Magic, Faith and Healing* (Glencoe, Ill.: Free Press, 1964), studied both disturbed and nondisturbed Pentecostals and found great differences between them. He could only conclude that their psychosis affected their religion rather than vice versa. William Wood in *Cultural and Personality Aspects of the Pentecostal Holiness Religion* (The Hague: Mouton and Loig, 1965) undertook a study to try to discover whether there was a "Pentecostal type" of personality. He used Rorschach tests exclusively. His findings seem very general and often confused, perhaps because of his overreliance on projective testing. But he does definitely conclude that there is no evidence of any correlation between mental disorder and Pentecostalism.

On the more positive side, studies have not only refuted the older contention that this is a form of mental illness but have shown positive correlations between *charismata* and mental health. Lincoln Vivier, in an unpublished doctoral dissertation on religion and psychiatry, entitled "Glossolalia," written at the University of Witwatershand in South Africa, reports on research in which he studied Pentecostals by means of batteries of psychological tests and psychiatric interviews. He found no indication of neurosis or latent psychosis in any of those studied. Nor did he find any evidence of dissociation, inordinate repression, or conversion hysteria—three classic elements of schizophrenia and clinical explanations of bizarre religious behavior. Rather he found them "more tolerant and humane in their interests" than a comparable group of non-Pentecostals. Stanley Plog used questionnaires and interviews with neo-Pentecostals in Los Angeles and found no evidence of disturbed mental states; rather he found them "very responsible and normally well controlled individuals." (reported in *J.S.S.R.*, VIII/2 [1969], 215 ff.) Nathan and Louise Gerrard studied a group of snakehandlers in West Virginia. They administered the Minnesota Multiphasic Personality Inventory test to both snake-handlers and conventional Protestants in the same area and described the results in their report, *Scrabble-Creek Folk* (unpublished, from Morris Harvey College, 1966). The tests were scored at the University of Minnesota and revealed that the snake-handlers were generally less defensive and less inclined toward denial and repression than the regular Protestants. Both groups were well within healthy limits.

Morton Kelsey includes in his book *Tongue Speaking* a vast number of cases where charismatic experience proved therapeutic. Fr. Kelsey is an Episcopal priest trained in Jungian psychology who was not personally involved in the Pentecostal movement at the time of his writing this book. He cites many cases where the experience of speaking in tongues alleviated long-standing mental disturbances. Thus the evidence is that charismatic experience, far from being a sign of mental difficulty, may in some cases be a sign of, or may increase, emotional health. In instances where it has been connected with disturbed states, the disturbance predates the Pentecostal experience. Yet I am sure the effort to link Pentecostalism with schizophrenia will die hard.

One reason it may never die is cited by Dr. Hine. She tells how the psychologists who scored the M.M.P.I. in the University of Minnesota for the Gerrard study were only told they had two groups—snake-handlers and conventional church members—but not which was which. After the scoring, all the clinicians assumed that the most abnormal batch must belong to the snake-handlers. The tests showed just the opposite. She cites other examples of bias against Pentecostals among professionals in the social sciences in the absence of any data. Almost all psychologists, she says, are predisposed, on no empirical grounds, to assume pathology in Pentecostals. In the circumstances, an objective social-scientific study of the Pentecostal movement may be impossible to carry out.

The classic psychoanalytic explanations for such phenomena are repression, dissociation, and conversion hysteria. None of the studies which used the appropriate tests found any abnormal tendencies in these directions among the Pentecostals. Some persons have suggested that Pentecostals are highly susceptible to suggestion and social pressure. Vivier specifically investigated these traits and found little support for the notion. The other common psychological explanation of speaking in tongues is that it is learned behavior, but Hine documents several incontestable cases where people received the gift of tongues with no previous knowledge of the phenomenon. Thus there seems to be little or no evidence that charismatic experience is a form of mental illness or can be "explained away" on psychological grounds.

Growing in the Fruits of the Spirit

There is probably more confusion about the relation of what Paul calls the "fruits" of the Spirit to the "gifts" of the Spirit than in any other area of charismatic theology. In Galatians, he lists the fruits of the Spirit as "love, joy, peace, patience, kindness, goodness, faithfulness, gentleness and self-control"—all those personal qualities that none of us have enough of and all want more of. This is where the confusion comes. I often hear people say something like "I don't want any of those funny things like tongues or prophecy, I want the 'greatest' gift which is love." But Paul never refers to love as a gift of the Spirit. The spiritual gifts are the various functions for building up the body of Christ—those of prophets, healers, speakers in tongues, interpreters, and so on. Paul always refers to love as a fruit of the Spirit, never as a gift.

This distinction between the fruits and the gifts is extremely important for two reasons. First, it helps to answer the question of how we can know more love and peace and joy. If they are fruits of the Spirit, this means that they are by-products of the Spirit's work. As a tree grows well, it produces good fruit. As the Spirit works within us, it produces the fruits of the Spirit of God. These ought not be sought by themselves, but as the result of the work of that Spirit whose fruit they are. If it is true that love is a fruit of the Spirit, then the way love can be increased is by increasing one's openness to the Spirit. How can that be done? The major way Paul recommends is by earnestly desiring spiritual gifts. To say I want the fruits of the Spirit without the gifts is like saying I want the fruit of the tree without the roots. For the roots nourish the tree, and it is exercise of gifts of the Spirit that nourishes the life of the Spirit within us and brings about its fruits.

I do not mean to imply that only people who speak in tongues are loving, peaceful, joyful, and so on—this is too obviously false to need refutation. There are other ways to release and be open to the Spirit than by the gifts we are discussing: faithfulness in prayer, attending to scripture, participation in the sacraments, love and service, all are expressions of the Spirit of God. But the special gifts of the Spirit are one of the major channels God has ordained for building up His people and carrying out His plan, and it would be foolish to neglect them. If a person sincerely seeks to increase the fruits of the Spirit, the primary way that increase can come is through increasing openness to the Spirit. And radical openness to the Spirit will eventually mean some consideration of the charismatic gifts. To those who seek the fruits the best advice is that of St. Paul: "Pursue love but earnestly desire spiritual gifts" (1 Cor. 14:1).

The distinction between fruits and gifts also helps to answer the basic question of how I know that my spiritual gifts are really spiritual. From Jesus and Paul and throughout Christian history the answer has been as we saw above: a tree is known by its fruit. It is not the intensity of emotion nor the flashiness of the *charismata* that validates a religious experience. There is only one test of whether a person's spiritual gifts are genuine, and that is whether they bear the fruits of the Spirit—whether their ministry edifies (i.e., builds up and renews) the body of Christ and enables others to share in the Kingdom of God. I have attended assemblies where there has been a great deal of apparent charismatic flash, but where bitterness and criticism have appeared rather than love, condemnation instead of peace, and grim determination rather than joy radiating from people's faces. All the seeming gifts and miracles in the world could not sanctify that assembly. In communities I have belonged to there were no wild displays of spiritual fireworks, but the people who come back week after week do so, they said, because the love of the Lord was there. St. Paul makes clear that a mechanical speaking in tongues without love is worthless. In the same context he says that the perfunctory doing of good works—even to giving away everything to feed the poor—has no value. All one's doings are to be judged by the fruit that they bear.

Paul is clear that there can be no setting in opposition of fruits and gifts. Those who are constantly drawn to displays of the spiritual gifts with no regard for a greater openness to the Spirit or an increase in the fruits, and those who seek the fruits of the Spirit according to their inclinations without seeking the Spirit that bears them, have both missed the point. There is an old Pentecostal word of wisdom to "seek the Giver and not the gifts." Persons to whom the gifts are ends in themselves forget that they are given by the Spirit of Christ to those who love and want to serve him. The same is true of the fruits: only if one seeks Christ and his Spirit can one harvest the fruits in their fullness. To those who seek, whether fruits or gifts, the advice of the Lord is always relevant: "Seek ye first the Kingdom of God and all these things will be added unto you."

Q. Why do these manifestations of the Spirit so seldom appear in the many regular church services which one assumes are attended by people who are thoughtfully and lovingly approaching the Lord?

A. Primarily I think because of a lack of openness and teaching. The Spirit is present but the expectation of spiritual gifts is absent. People who come for confirmation—in the Episcopal church—are not taught that when the bishop lays hands upon them they will probably speak an unknown language! (They are probably subtly taught that were they to do any such thing they would be taken away in an ambulance.) Thus they do not expect spiritual gifts. Yet these sometimes appear anyway. I have met several Roman Catholics who told me that when they were confirmed as children they had powerful spiritual experiences with charismatic gifts. But since they did not understand what was happening and did not know what to do, and since there was no community in which to express these gifts, they soon forgot about them until they encountered the same experience years later in the charismatic movement. I know an Episcopal priest who is generally opposed to the charismatic movement, who told me that when the bishop laid hands on him at ordination he spoke in tongues. But not since. It is lack of teaching and openness that inhibits this sort of expression in "regular church services." Where teaching and an open attitude prevail, charismatic gifts begin to flourish. I know of Catholic and Episcopal parishes (and I am sure there are Lutheran and Reformed ones) where people are taught about spiritual gifts, and receive and exercise them with decency and order in the context of regular worship.

Q. Will you say something about the interpretation of tongues? Is it necessary? Who interprets and how is it done? When a whole congregation speaks in tongues are they necessarily interpreted?

A. I think it is extremely important to make a distinction between the use of the gift of tongues to renew the individual and to edify an assembly. Paul says that the primary function of tongues is to renew the person (1 Cor. 14:4). If it is to renew the church by instructing it, there must be interpretation. When a person merely speaks in tongues individually, the Spirit flows through him and he is renewed, but his mind and the surrounding assembly are not instructed. There is a distinction between the use of tongues to renew a person spiritually by allowing the Spirit to flow through them and the use of tongues to deliver a message. In the first case, no interpretation is necessary; the communion is between the individual and God. But if there is a message to the assembly there must be interpretation, otherwise it obviously cannot be understood. Thus no one should speak a message in tongues to an assembly unless it is interpreted, but one can pray in tongues to oneself and God to renew oneself without an interpretation (1 Cor. 14:28).

Now I would go beyond this to suggest that the whole assembly may act together as one person and pray together in tongues (usually sing together in tongues in praise of God), so that the Spirit may flow freely through the whole community. This is the first use of tongues—for spiritual renewal. Since it is not for instruction, no interpretation is necessary, or perhaps possible. This practice of a whole assembly singing and praying as one in the Spirit is an extension of the first use of tongues from individuals to communities. Paul does not speak about this one way or another.

As to how it is done I cannot say much. I have rarely, if

ever, experienced the gift of interpretation. In the communities I have belonged to, almost all edification is through the gift of prophecy rather than tongues and interpretation. I suspect it is like prophecy. One senses the words welling up inside oneself. Usually there is what the Pentecostals call an "anointing," that is, one feels a pulsing of energy within. (Jer. 23:29 "Is not my word like fire, says the Lord, and like a hammer which breaks the rock in pieces?") If one resists speaking, the pulsing increases as one fights against it. Usually one begins with just a sentence or two, and as one yields to it a fully formed prophecy comes out. But the real test of any such message, whether prophecy or interpretation, is whether or not it renews the group. It must be received and judged by the community as word from the Lord and not just a nice idea someone happened to have. The community must be built up by what is spoken. The tree is known by its fruits.

Q. I don't understand why speaking in tongues is a gift if no one understands. I can see it might mean something to the person, but how about the rest of the people?

A. I think it can still be a gift even if no one understands, because it is not primarily intended for the understanding (that would be wisdom, knowledge, or prophecy). There is more to man than the mind, and speaking in tongues can renew a person at all levels of life—not only the cognitive—when he is open for the Spirit to flow through him at more than just the intellectual level. It does not mean anything cognitive to other people or to the person himself (it is not supposed to; that is not what it is for) unless there is interpretation.

Q. All this talk using the words "supernatural" and "miracle" creates a semantic problem for lots of us. The term "superstition" popped into my mind. It seems most appropriate.

A. This is a large area. Obviously we cannot discuss here the whole philosophical problem of miracles. I think you are right: there is a semantic problem. I myself do not like the words "supernatural" or "miracle"; it seems almost impossible to come clear philosophically about what one means by them, because the eighteenth-century definition is still with us, when the world was seen as a vast machine running by iron-clad laws of nature, and "miracle" was a violation of these laws. Nowadays the idea of iron-clad laws of nature does not make much sense; few modern philosophers of science would accept it. Yet it persists, and the discussion of miracles always gets bogged down in discussion of whether the "laws of nature" can be broken. I don't think we can come clear on this notion of laws of nature—in fact, I don't think there are such things in the strict eighteenth-century sense. But this does not solve the problem of miracles, it only makes the word more difficult to use. The same is true of the word "supernatural."

Why then do I use them? Because there is a tendency to solve semantic problems by redefinition. I say one thing and people immediately redefine what I've said to make it more acceptable. Then it ceases to mean what I intended. They think "he doesn't really mean *that*. He doesn't really mean God directly healed that person, he means that nature or coincidence created an anomaly." The truth is, I really mean that God directly healed that person! I use such outrageous words (to present sensibility) as miracle and supernatural because they *are* outrageous. They are harder to instantly redefine. They jar people enough to make them sit up and take notice of the possibility of such occurrences.

This is all I can say here, since a philosophical discussion of miracles is beyond the scope of this book. In the charismatic movement, lots of outrageous and jarring and unpredictable things happen—people are healed, prophecies delivered, discernment exercised. How these are understood (as "miracle," "anomaly," "chance," etc.) is a question of faith and philosophy beyond our present range. That they happen and that they bear certain good fruit is a fact of the charismatic movement which all must face with as much openness and objectivity as they can muster.

Chapter 4

EXPERIENCE OF THE SPIRIT

What Is Your Experience?

People are both attracted and repelled by the charismatic movement. They are attracted by the presence of God, by the experience of love and peace and joy they hear about, by the excitement of mighty signs and large assemblies. They are uneasy about exactly the same things: skeptical about the presence of God, repelled by the idea of talking in a language one does not know, doubtful about the miraculous. Therefore the best way to answer the question about the relevancy of the Pentecostal experience is to ask, relevancy for whom? How we answer the question of what this might mean to someone depends on who it is. Here are four positions church people today often find themselves in and what the charismatic movement might mean to each.

1. Let us call the first the normal church member. This is the long-standing church goer who is relatively satisfied with the way things are. The problems belong to someone else. Such persons may have grown up in the church and may feel quite comfortable about it. They are probably put off by the classic Pentecostal insistence that there is something lacking in their faith. They are not aware of any lack; they feel quite content. This may be a problem. When a person feels self-satisfied and content—whether it be a stuffy Episcopalian, a fanatical evan-

gelical, or an overzealous Pentecostal—then he has ceased to be responsive to God. No one, Pentecostal or other, has arrived at such degree of spirituality that he can rest content. God always has more in store.

Such a person may feel satisfied—oddly enough—because he does not realize fully the love of God for him. And the Pentecostal who judges and condemns his Christianity is doing the exact opposite of what should be done. A person who is content may need love and not judgment, for he may not sense at all that God, in His love, has more to give him, or that he stands in need of it. The question ought not to be: What is the least I can get away with spiritually? It ought to be, rather: What is the most God wants for me? The point is not whether for the normal church member the doing of one's "religious duty" is enough. Enough for what? Perhaps sufficient to satisfy himself, but, surely not enough to satisfy the love of God for him. The regular church member has obviously received a great deal through his attention to the Bible, sacraments, and the work of the church. But God has more.

Some classical Pentecostal teaching assumes that when one is baptized in the Spirit one throws over all that belonged to a normal pre-Pentecostal church life. As we have seen, this is because these Pentecostals took over from evangelical pietism a notion of the Christian life as a series of crises. The understanding served them well in their evangelical environment. But I am suggesting another way of understanding the Christian life and the place of the baptism of the Holy Spirit within it. It seems to me that the Christian life is a matter of slow growth—evolution if you will. This consists not in throwing over what went before but in deepening and appropriating it in new ways. The Christian life begins at baptism. The New Testament says that at baptism one "dies to sin and rises to newness of life," and part of this life is the reception of the Holy Spirit. But obviously this is a potential which must be allowed to grow and be integrated into one's life. No one—whether right after baptism or after a hundred years of Christian living—has totally died to sin. No one, not even the most mature Pentecostal in spite of his special gifts, has totally received the Spirit into all areas of his life. This must wait till the Kingdom has finally come. Rather, the original baptism gives one a potential which must gradually grow and spread like leaven in a loaf.

Christian life is a continual series of experiences that deepen this potential. Every time a person takes the bread and wine, his commitment to Jesus Christ is renewed; when he hears the message of Christianity preached or reads the Bible, his faith is replenished; every time he repents of sin and seeks forgiveness, his Christian life is strengthened (even if he must repent again the very same day). When people are confirmed, when they make a self-conscious commitment of their lives to Jesus Christ, when they undergo some dramatic religious experience (if they do), this does not change the basic fact of their baptism and previous life in Christ, but rather deepens and expands what was there.

So it is with the gifts of the Spirit. They are there in potential all along. That is why I am uncomfortable at basing too much theology on the term "baptism in the Holy Spirit." It implies that the Spirit was not present earlier. I prefer "release of the Spirit." For what spiritual gifts do is to release the Spirit present since baptism and give the person a new openness to it. Baptism in the Spirit does not demand that one suddenly condemn as unspiritual everything that has gone before. Rather, it is one more event by which a Christian life is further deepened and renewed.

The charismatic movement does not judge the normal, faithful, but noncharismatic churchgoer. But it holds out to him the possibility of a further deepening and enlivening of all he holds dear in his Christian profession. Baptism in the Holy Spirit is one more stage in that long, slow process of incorporating God's love which begins at original baptism and will not end until the Last Day. It does not imply that the Spirit has previously been absent—only that it is now being more fully released into one's life.

2. A second group in the church I call the alienated Christians. These are people who find themselves moving more and more toward the fringe of church life. It holds less interest for them; they find themselves attending infrequently where once they were quite loyal. Generally these people define their faith in terms of some external act. For some, it has meant intellectual assent to Christian doctrine; for others, a certain style of behavior—performing or not performing certain kinds of action. Gradually they have found a gap opening up between what they professed and where they lived. The two worlds—that of their belief and that of their everyday life—cease to hang together. Usually this is referred to as a crisis of faith, yet it is not a crisis of intellectual belief. Few people find themselves in this position because philosophical argument has convinced them that Christianity was false. Rather it is a crisis of experience. The experiential heart of faith has gradually disappeared, and only the shell of belief or activity remains.

These alienated Christians are often nostalgic for their faith; it continues to fascinate and attract them. But they are grimly realistic. "You can't go back," they say. "You can't go home any more." I have met many clergy, laymen, and church officers alike in this position, looking wistfully backward to some supposed time of "simple faith," yet dogmatically determined to live in the present, which they deeply feel means living without faith.

I think much of the present interpretation of this phenomenon of alienation within the church is misconceived. Often religious pundits make it seem like an intellectual problem. Some current theologians (who rarely discuss the hard problems of the philosophy of science) suggest that since the modern world is formed by technology and science, faith is well-nigh impossible.* The solution, then, is to repackage the faith intellectually. Wrap it in a new intellectual dress cut from the cloth of the present age. This assumes that the problem is one of understanding—that people simply do not comprehend gospel language any more. The only hope is to translate it into a more contemporary tongue.

Obviously, if the gospel is to communicate, it must speak a language people can grasp, but the assumption that the problem of alienation arises from deficient mental comprehension seems too facile. Perhaps it is no coincidence that this interpretation is argued for the most part by professors (like myself) who give the world of the intellect a certain priority. I suspect that the dilemma of alienation within the church is really one of experience, that people's separation from their faith reflects what is in fact a far deeper alienation of inward personal experience from the external self—the façade of behavior and ideas we push around ahead of ourselves. The alienated Christian is one who has begun with an externalized definition of faith as assent or behavior. It is easy, then, for the outer man to go through the motions of belief and action while the inner person is devoid of experiences that nourish faith and a vital existence. The attempts to confront this problem by trying to appeal to the mind with new reconstructions of Christian theology, or by laying on heavier moral exhortations to greater involvement in Christian action—these make it worse rather than better. They treat the symptom, not the disease. They appeal to the outer man, merely, while the difficulty arises from a division of the outer from the inner self—a separation that comes about because there has been too much concentration in the church on

---

*Rudolf Bultmann, *Kerygma and Myth* (New York: Harper & Row, 1961); Thomas Altizer and William Hamilton, *Radical Theology and the Death of God* (Indianapolis: Bobbs-Merrill, 1966); Langdon Gilkey, *Naming the Whirlwind* (Indianapolis; Bobbs-Merrill, 1969).

intellectual reconstruction and moral activity without an equal focus on the roots of believing and acting.

If this is at least a partially correct analysis (and from conversations with many in this position I sincerely believe it is), then the charismatic movement or something like it may hold the only cure. As ought to be clear from what I have said so far, it does not neglect theology and ethics, but it also recreates some of the experiences out of which Christian belief and morality arose. Yet it does not create them just for the sake of experience; I do not believe that the gap between our inner and outer selves can be bridged simply by wallowing in vivid sensations, for these would be as hard to integrate into the self as is the purely external behavior of habitual—"normal"—life. The charismatic movement recreates particular kinds of experience which naturally give rise to Christian faith and action: awareness of the love and presence of God and of Christian community. Thus the disharmony people feel between what they believe and what they live inwardly is overcome, not by hacking down their beliefs to fit their truncated inner life, but by enabling them to experience what they believe.

One example from many will make this clear. I remember a Roman Catholic priest who, like many in the church, found himself in an orbit that would take him not only out of the ministry but out of the church and out of Christianity entirely. He suddenly woke one morning in a cell of a room in a cold, brick, fortresslike rectory and realized that he was totally alienated from the world around him. He was celibate; most of his acquaintances were married. He lived virtually alone; most people he knew had close friends. In his official capacity he said things and performed actions the meaning of which he had trouble making clear to himself and those around him. He wondered if this was the best use of his time and his life.

He resolved to become more involved and plunged into several community service projects. There he found people whose assumptions were even further removed from his own. The work provided some relief from the weight of his official role, but he could not relate it to his "vocation" and so it further alienated him from himself. He entered counseling—for though there was nothing psychologically wrong with his personality, he could not bear the strain of holding so many conflicting worlds together in one mind.

In this state he came to a charismatic community. He was repelled, but kept coming. He saw there a people whose liturgy was an actual celebration of what they felt and lived. Here were priests and laymen whose apostolate in the world was not a refuge from their vocation as Christians but flowed naturally out of their call as the people of God. In this community one was not alone or isolated, but lived in a world of shared experience. As he continued to come, he noticed the greatest change at the point of his greatest sense of separation from his tradition: the scriptures. This is true of most people in the charismatic movement. Scripture had made little sense to him. The larger part of the New Testament he simply let alone. He dwelt on the Gospel pictures of Jesus and forgot about the remainder. All of a sudden he discovered two things about the Bible. First, he found that what it described was not something long past and dead; rather these things were happening to him and those around him. Second, it often seemed as if the words had been written directly to him, so relevant were they.

All the decisions of this priest about his life are not settled—they never are, that is what it means to walk by faith—but through his involvement in the charismatic movement his alienation was overcome. The story is typical of many I have met. A large number of those who have come to the community in St. Paul were on the last round of an orbit that was taking them out of the church altogether.

3. A third group I will call the exhausted believers. These are not people who feel alienated; rather they are passionately

committed to the church. For them, faith is synonymous with involvement: the true Christian, they feel, is deeply involved. Thus they have thrown themselves into every project, worked themselves to the bone. Suddenly they are overweary. Their resources are spent. They have neglected essential things. Their mind and bodies have short-circuited and blown their fuses; suddenly they feel tired, and the dread sense of boredom begins to bubble up. Life looks flat. I have seen lives which were once like sparkling wine thus turn to stale, flat soda water.

Often when this happens they drop out; they take a "rest" which never ends. Or they try to manufacture the excitement they once felt naturally: they work hard to get more people involved, to gin up the group psyche, to replace the vitality they once had. Or they propose new and more fantastic projects, hoping this will rekindle the fire. Others lapse into a joyless determination to hang in there, to be martyrs to the cause, and stoic resignation replaces love and peace and joy as the highest Christian virtues.

What is amiss? Not the projects themselves—they are all good. What goes wrong is that people try to do them on their own. No one has bothered to ask if they were what the Lord wanted doing, no one waited on His guidance and His power. The projects were doubtless all valuable (in some sense), but they were man's undertakings—things man thought up, planned out, tried to accomplish with only a nod in God's direction. No one asked the Lord in at the beginning; at best they piously asked a blessing on matters already planned, and hoped He would pull them out at the end if the going got rough. People are exhausted because they rely on their own steam and wisdom, and no one has enough of either to do what needs doing.

At issue here is a fundamental judgment about the nature of man. The weary believer who begins with a definition of Christianity as involvement, starts with an external definition both of man and of faith: a person is what he does! I would say No. A person's actions are a reflection of what he *is.* This was the way of the Lord. Much of Jesus' teaching focuses on the inner man. He condemned the Pharisees not because they were immoral; they were, after all, the strictest keepers of the law. What he said was that this correct outward behavior did not accurately reflect their inward state. They concentrated on the external. "Cleanse the inside of the cup," he tells them, "and everything will be clean." A tree that is sound within will produce good fruit. While a bad tree may produce some good fruit, Jesus implies in Matt 7:16–20 that ultimately its fruit will be rotten. One does not try to graft fruit-bearing scions onto dying stock; rather, one fertilizes the tree so that it will naturally produce. Yet some in the church, when they feel it is not producing enough good works, try to graft on it external appeals for more activity rather than giving the church itself more nourishment so that it can in the natural course of things produce better fruit. Jesus begins with the inner man, not to deny concern for moral actions, but out of the profound insight that man's activity springs from and reflects his inner life.

One reason people get exhausted is that they take on more activity than their inner life can support. But the release of the Spirit through the exercise of spiritual gifts provides more nourishment and power than any human being can use. Even the most spiritually mature charismatic has tapped only a fraction of the vitality available to him through the indwelling Spirit. Paul says that the Spirit who lives within us is the same Spirit that raised Jesus from the dead. Just think about that for a moment! We have within us the power that conquers even death itself, that last enemy in Paul's words. But even the most mature in the Spirit bring into realization only a fraction of that energy. Most of us are so weak in faith that we do not come close, even with the spiritual gifts.

The charismatic movement starts with a definition of man

which begins from the inside and works out. It is not another project to take on—another set of duties to add to an already too-full schedule. Rather it is a reorienting of all life out from a common center, a reversing of priorities so that the roots are fertilized and helped to grow, well before any effort is made to harvest; the foundation is laid before the building is built. The life in the Spirit is not a schizophrenia, a dualism in one's existence, so that one tries to live many lives at once. In the life in the Spirit one is freed from taking on more than one can do and empowered to do all one takes on.

4. Finally, the last type of person is the sincere seeker, those who are outside the church looking in. The subject of conversion to Christianity can be difficult. It smacks of intolerance and bigotry and coercion. The Spirit never coerces anybody, and those who attempt to force people cannot be doing the Spirit's work. But it does tenderly seek to draw people within direct range of the experience of God's love. And this love is seen most clearly in the face of Jesus Christ. Thus many people come to know the Lord and His love through the charismatic movement who have been untouched by other types of appeal. Many adults came to the community in St. Paul who had not been to church in years, or who had not even been raised religiously. Many young people came who had dabbled in everything from drugs to the occult, searching for a faith. The movement attracts people to the Lord in the same way the early church did, not only by holding out the gospel but also by demonstration of the power of the Spirit and of Christian community. At least in the mainline Protestant and Catholic traditions, it holds out the full range of Christian experience—the gospel word, the sacramental life, life in the Spirit, the community of faith—for all to see and to judge.

Like all true Christianity, the charismatic movement is in the world though not of it. To the extent that it is in the world, it obviously partakes of human sin and limitation and does not hold out the love of God so clearly that all can see it. As a matter of fact, a great deal of harm has been done by overzealous Pentecostal types who have forgotten the theological fact that conversion is the Spirit's work (not ours) and the Pauline injunction to "make love your aim"; who have set about to apply charismatic coercion rather than holding out God's love. More husbands, wives, children, fellow church members, and others have been turned off by this than by any other factor. On the other hand, week after week in these communities people come with their skepticism on their sleeve and are overwhelmed by the power and love of God.

The Secret of the Spiritual Life

The day of Pentecost is the prototype of all Pentecostal experience. On that day Peter instructed the people in how to enter into a deeper life in the Spirit. He begins by telling them what God has done in Jesus of Nazareth. He describes the mighty acts of God that reveal His love for men and His plan for creation. The gospel is grounded in the divine love. This is the most important thing we can know about God—that He loves all persons and wants to draw them deeper into union with Him. The gospel begins with the love of God, and that is where the Pentecostal experience begins too.

Some people have trouble in beginning here. They think of God in ways that keep them from seeing Him as a loving Father. Many who have been brought up in the church think of Him as a cosmic scorekeeper, whether sitting up in heaven with a big book or more intangibly, somehow keeping very accurate accounts. Every time they do something wrong, He marks it down. This view gets them uptight. It is hard to think of Him as a loving Father if you are always afraid He's checking up on you. Others think of God as far away, a distant force, a vague cosmic source. It is difficult to imagine something so abstract as loving and caring. Throughout the Gospels Jesus pictures God as a loving Father, and it is only in the context of a God who loves and cares and knows even the number of hairs on our head, that the work of the Spirit makes any sense.

People who think of God as a scorekeeper say, "I am not worthy to receive the very Spirit of God." Those who think of Him as far away say, "It's foolish to suppose that God Himself would work in and through something as insignificant as one person." The work of the Spirit, fortunately, does not depend on our feelings about God but on His feelings about us. In Jesus God has shown as clearly as can be His intention to love all men and draw them into union with Himself.

Which brings up the next point in Peter's sermon on the day of Pentecost. How is this love of God appropriated into our lives? In answer to this question Peter says, "Repent, and be baptized . . . and you shall receive the gift of the Holy Spirit for the promise is made to you and to your children . . . and everyone whom the Lord our God calls." Repentance and baptism are the ways in which the love of God is appropriated. At baptism we are committed to follow Jesus Christ as Lord. We renew that commitment every time we say the Creed and take the sacrament of his body and blood. Explicit commitment to Jesus Christ as Lord is a necessary prerequisite for the exercise of spiritual gifts. This commitment means a willingness to follow him and do his will. The Holy Spirit is his spirit. It is given to strengthen his church and carry out his plan. There is no use in giving the Spirit to those who are not willing to go where he wants them to go and do what he want them to do. The gifts of the Spirit take place in the context of an explicit affirmation of the Lordship of Jesus Christ. Paul expresses this by insisting that the Holy Spirit is also the Spirit of Jesus Christ. The Pentecostals say that Jesus is the baptizer in the Spirit. The point is that only in the context of commitment to Christ can the gifts of the Spirit be exercised.

The same is true of repentance. This does not mean simply feeling sorry for our mistakes. It is easy to feel sorry; it's not easy really to measure our lives by God's will. The Greek word *metanoia*, which we translate as repentance, means a reordering of one's whole life in the direction of God's will. It means changes in how we think, feel, and perceive as well as how we behave. It means struggling to stop doing things our own way all the time and letting God do them His way. It means resigning ourselves to the will of God.

All this boils down to one thing. The classic spiritual writers of the church call it resignation: a total giving over of one's life into the hands of God, a radical trust in His providence regardless of circumstances. This is the attitude of one who can say in the midst of the most terrible tragedy, "All things work together for good for those who love God." It is best exemplified by a popular but mistaken translation in the book of Job on the part of the Authorized (King James) Version of the Bible, where Job is quoted as saying "though He slay me, yet will I trust Him." It is what Paul was talking about when he wrote to the Philippians "I have learned in whatever state I am to be content, I know what it is like to be beaten down and I know what it is like to succeed. In every situation I have learned the secret of being full and being hungry, of succeeding and being poor. I can do everything through him who gives me the strength" (Phil. 4:12–13).

Openness is a precondition for experience. Many people miss significant experiences in life because they are not open to them. We have all met persons who are so convinced that life is cruel that they cannot rejoice in the good things that happen to them; or those who are so optimistic and cheerful that they do not see the sufferings of others or let themselves be touched by their sorrows. I have gone mountain-climbing with people who missed the beauty of the wildflowers or the freshness of the pine trees or the chattering of the chipmunks and the voices of the birds because they were too busy worrying about whether it would rain or we would make the campsite before dark. These concerns kept them from being open to—and thus experiencing—the joys of nature around them.

So with spiritual gifts, openness is a precondition to the experience. What ancient spiritual writers called resignation is a form of openness and responsiveness to the will of God. It means putting aside our own plans and ideas and wishes and concentrating instead on His will and presence. For most of us this kind of responsiveness to God's Spirit is the hardest possible thing—so hard as to be almost inconceivable. We are used to taking account of ourselves and our own sense of logic and priorities first, and everyone else—God included—second or third. We are used to listening first to our own desires, our own plans, our own best interest, and only after fully guaranteeing what we imagine is our security are we willing to listen to others, including God.

The reasons for this have to do in part with the nature of man and in part with our society. We live in the ethos of the self-made man. Our political ideology, the images of our mass media, sometimes even the rhetoric of our preachers, encourage us to rely on our own strength, take pride in what we do, and be our own boss. It is true, of course, that there may sometimes be a neurotic weakness of dependency which masquerades as humility and crops out in the grown person who must rely on alcohol or drugs for the constant reassurance of surrogate parents to get him through the day. But the apostles were not such people. They were vigorous and active, they faced death and stood up to emperors, and yet—and indeed this was the source of their strength—they acknowledged their total dependence upon God.

We like to take pride in ourselves. It is the mark of Adam upon us and enables us to recognize ourselves in the story of that man who wanted to be like God. Our culture reinforces this tendency with its Horatio Alger images and its mythical figures of rugged individualism. The gospel does not ask that we be weak and emaciated, but that we be open and responsive to the Spirit. Images of surrender and humility seem so passive to us; they appear foolish and evoke scorn. But as St. Paul reminds us, the foolishness of man is often the power of God.

The charismatic movement says that the power of God wants to move through us, making us not weak but strong. But for this to be possible we must be open to it, we must learn to be responsive. This means turning from interest in ourselves, from the fetish of our own security, from the endless spinning of bigger and better daydreams, and absolute confidence in our own logic. It means putting our life at His disposal. In the culture of the self-made man which exalts self-interest as a primary virtue this is not easy to do. But it must be done if we are to develop a sensitivity to the Spirit at least equal to—if possible, greater than—our impulsive obedience to our own egos.

And this brings up another reason why, in this society, we find it so difficult to respond to God's Spirit. We are desensitized. This was inevitable, given the development of mass communications. Every night on the seven o'clock news I am confronted with more human misery than I can possibly comprehend or react to: a flood in Pakistan, an earthquake in South America, the death toll from Southeast Asia or some other area. "Hundreds and thousands dead . . . millions homeless," the newscaster says in deadpan voice. He does not weep, nor do I. How can I conceive of even a thousand dead? All my family wiped out? That is only a fraction. My whole neighborhood gone, or my whole city? My power to imagine the concomitant suffering fails, my compassion has long been stretched so taut that the thread breaks; my empathy shuts down. Yet night after night I am subjected to this bombardment of misery from around the world. Thus I have become desensitized. I remember very clearly a night when, sitting before the TV screen, my mind, against the straining of heart and will, ceased to be able to differentiate the newsreels of Vietnam from the war movies of Hollywood I had watched as a kid on Saturday mornings. Try as I might, I could no longer really see the suffering of the war as real. I had become desensitized.

We are calloused not only because overexposure to suffering has short-circuited our compassion, but also because our style of life has hidden local suffering from us. Since we are largely unaware of pain in our lives, the pain of others fails to evoke any kindred response. The sick in their moans and contortions are whisked off to hospitals, where regulations or drugs often shield us from seeing them in any intense discomfort. The old are hidden away in nursing homes, to be made up and wheeled out for inspection on Sunday afternoons. Even the dead are so transformed that the look and smell of death eludes our senses. This is what it means to be well-off. It need not mean being a millionaire, living in a thirty-room mansion, riding in a limousine. But it means being shielded from the rhythm of pain and healing, of struggle and victory, that is life. Many in our society are too comfortable—not because they have too much money or too many possessions, but because they have healing without first having pain, and victory without overcoming any obstacles.

The desensitized, insulated person who has lost awareness of anything beyond the world of his own family, friends, and job loses the ability to tell good from bad, right from wrong. The bad becomes simply the unpleasant; it is synonymous with what makes one feel uncomfortable. The desensitized person, living in a world built of pillows in which he feels totally at home, loses the initiative to respond to challenges and take risks. The shrug of a shoulder represents his basic posture. "Why bother?" he thinks to himself time and time again. "I might lose what I already have." More and more frequently on my local news report (which comes out of New York City) there is the story of someone who was beaten, robbed, or killed while his fellow citizens stood around passively and watched. The media continue to run these stories—not, I'm afraid, in the naïve hope that they may awaken the atrophied powers of compassion in their audience, but perhaps partly because such occurrences are ongoing parables of life in the land of the desensitized.

Those who see themselves under the sign of the self-made man in whom pride of achievement is the highest value, those whose empathy has been smothered under the heaps of human suffering piled up by the mass media, those whose capacity to grasp life with something more than the fingertips has been dissolved in the world of their own comfort—these have lost the openness and responsiveness without which there can be no life in the Spirit. Responsiveness, suppleness to the Spirit of God is the secret of the spiritual life, but it is a secret forever lost to those who cannot venture beyond the walls of their own ego. There are, however, two experiences which can break down the blocks we have hewn out of the rock of our selfishness: these are suffering and the encounter with spiritual gifts.

Many Pentecostals do not like to speak of suffering. They want to give the impression that the Christian life is all sweetness and light. But the Bible says of Jesus that "although he was a son, still he learned obedience through what he suffered" (Heb 5:8). A disciple is not above his master. Even though Jesus was the Son of God, he had to obey, to surrender, to be humble in suffering. So it is with us. When things do not go the way we want, when we come into pain and affliction, then the stubborn root of our selfishness is revealed. Rather than surrendering to the Lord and saying, "All right, Lord, if this is your will, I'll accept it," we rail against it, we cry out, we say, "Lord, why aren't you dealing with me the way I want you to?" It is easy to say you trust God when things are going well, for it is easy to confuse trust in God with our own satisfaction that everything is as we want it to be. When things go badly—when sickness strikes, when business fails and the future closes down

—then we can see clearly whether we really trust in God or only worship at the shrine of our own good fortune. Thus suffering teaches us, as it taught the Lord, to be humble, to break our will over the anvil of His divine good pleasure. If we can be humble and trusting and thankful before the Lord when things are going badly, then we are supple enough in the Spirit to be His instruments.

This is the secret of the spiritual life. It is easy to say precisely because it is the hardest thing to do: to let go of our selves and have only that part of our will left that is necessary to complete His purposes. This is what must happen if the Lord is to work through us. We must ignore our plans, our ideas, our dreams. We must be willing to give up everything we treasure—success, prestige, reputation—if it should stand between ourselves and His will. It is a lifelong process of bearing the cross, that symbol of total self-denial, total giving of oneself over to the will of God. For most of us this is achieved mainly in the inferno of suffering. It is not because God is vindictive or angry that we suffer; it is a measure of our own stubborness and not His hostility that we finally turn to Him only when we are so broken that we can see no other alternative. It is only when we see nothing *we* can do that we give ourselves over to God. He does not want it so, but our pride makes it so. Usually only pain is strong enough to break down our defiant determination to rely on ourselves and teach us the lesson of surrender and humility. Without such lessons there is little life in the Spirit.

The Spirit is released as we give ourselves over to God's working. He does not coerce us, He does not overpower us; *we* must surrender to Him. This is where the gifts of the Spirit come in. One way to surrender to the Holy Spirit is to allow it to work through us in the exercising of spiritual gifts. Speaking in tongues is not very important in itself, but yielding to the Holy Spirit and allowing it to work through us in this way begins the process by which we open more and more to that Spirit. It also shows us what is at issue in yielding to the more important gifts, and this is perhaps why such a little thing often produces tremendous results. For many people, speaking in tongues is the first time they have yielded a little of themselves into God's hands. It is the first time they have said they were willing to go all the way with the Lord and meant it! In response to this openness, the Spirit really floods their lives in an overwhelming way. For others, who have been radically open to the Spirit in other ways, letting themselves go in tongues may not produce such a torrential experience. But it will speed them on their way to a deeper yielding to God in other areas.

Speaking in tongues also reveals what is at stake for us in our relation to God. People often balk at tongues. They say in effect, "Yes, Lord, I want to have love and joy and be able to heal people, but don't give me any of that speaking in tongues." It does appear foolish, but its very foolishness is the key to its power. What is a person in effect saying when he says he doesn't want to speak in tongues, even after he understands that it is a gift of God? Usually he is saying, "I don't want to appear foolish." For many it is a matter of sheer pride. People will laugh at them.

For others it is a question of self-image. It is very important to them always to be in control of themselves in a situation. To let go—to let God take charge—to trust God or someone else —is a major step and they draw back. For some (particularly academic types like myself) it is a matter of understanding. They do not like things they cannot comprehend. Mystery frightens them. Since speaking in tongues appears so irrational, they will not involve themselves in something they are unable to figure out.

In all these there is the same dialectic of pride and surrender. Because to speak in tongues seems so foolish, our fear of it forces us to examine how much our pride keeps us from surrendering totally to God. If a person is afraid of what others will think, he will not be as bold as the Lord wants him to be. If a person must always be in control, he will not trust the Lord to lead him into areas where only He knows the way. If a person must understand everything, he will not be open to the Lord to work mighty things beyond man's comprehension. The little gift of tongues throws into relief what is really involved in more important spheres of Christian living: Do we trust God enough, are we responsive enough to let Him do anything He wants with us, even if it means appearing foolish, even if it means things we don't understand?

This is why this little gift can bear so much fruit. God, the loving Father, will not do anything to hurt us. Most of us do not really believe that. But we can learn from experience. Many people who have feared yielding to the gift of tongues learn from their initial experience—when they find it did not produce all that they feared, but rather a great deal of good—that God does love them and lead them, and they are much more open to follow His guidance and much bolder to do what He wants. Yielding to tongues has helped them to grow in the Spirit.

Perhaps the best analogy to the release of the Spirit is water flowing through a pipe. If you close up the pipe, the water will stagnate. If you open the pipe and allow the water to flow freely through it, it will cool the pipe and there will always be a fresh flow. Exercising the gifts of the Spirit, speaking and singing in tongues in praise to the Lord, praying with power for healing, following His discernment, all allow the Spirit to flow freely through us and out of us into the world. So often when God pours His Spirit into us, we dam it up and it stagnates. The exercise of spiritual gifts allows it to flow freely and work freely.

These, then, are the two major functions of the spiritual gifts in the individual's life. First, they are a release of the Spirit, long dammed up. The person surrenders to the Spirit, gives his life (or part of it) over to it, and this allows the Spirit to work. God longs to work in the life of all His children, but they must be open and responsive to Him.

Second, this is an initiation into a deeper life in the Spirit. It is not an end but the beginning of a more profound contact, which requires total openness. Exercising spiritual gifts gets us over the threshold of this deeper life. Commitment to a deeper life is a commitment to let the Lord have His way, for a change, and is dramatized and expressed in the willingness to let Him use us. The Spirit does not want to lie dormant in us, does not want to be only partially at work. God's Spirit is active and lively. To sum up once more: for His plan to be carried out men must be brought within the orbit of His love, and His Spirit must be released into all the world. This happens only through people, who are His body in the world. When they are open and pliant in His hands, then and only then can He truly use them in His service. Exercising the gifts of the Spirit is a beginning toward greater responsiveness, greater release of the power of the Spirit, and fuller participation in the plan of God.

Q. Is not the Holy Spirit present in the everyday things of life? Do we not sometimes seek it too far away from our own immediate experiences?

A. Surely God is present everywhere. That's part of what it means to say he is the Creator and Preserver of all that is. But we can only begin to perceive Him everywhere, if we have first had contact with Him in some specific human way. For most if not all of us it is because we first experience God in particular ways—in the Bible, the sacraments, the life of Jesus, the fellowship of the church, a friend or two—that we are enabled to know Him as being present universally, in all aspects of life. Concentration on spiritual gifts which may seem remote from everyday experience is not meant to negate the universal presence of God, but to enable people to experience Him in a particular area so that they may in the end be opened to finding Him everywhere.

Q. I want to go back to your image of the spigot and the pipe. We agree that Christian life ought not to stagnate and that the Spirit should flow freely. How about people in the church who have closed up the spigot and removed the handle, who are just determined not to grow or change or be open at all to anything?

A. This is an extremely hard question. Often it can only be dealt with in a pastoral way, one to one—not in a large public discussion. I have tried to stay away from being judgmental. But when one loves the church and longs for its renewal and the deepening of its life and yet sees people sitting in the pews totally closed to any growth, there is great sadness and pain. Not only in our hearts but also in the heart of God. God loves these people too; I have tried to stress the love of God. But your question raises the point that there is also the judgment of God. When the love of God is refused it becomes a judgment. This goes back to what I have just finished saying—why it's so hard to encounter the kind of people you describe. It seems that only suffering will break them down enough to open them to God's love. One prays that it need not be so but one also knows that, when one prays for them to be more open, perhaps the only way this can happen is for them to suffer and so be humbled and thus opened to God and his love.

No one wants another person to have pain, particularly if he has suffered himself. But the love of God when closed off becomes judgment; only through judgment can some people learn the lesson of love. This is what the letter to the Hebrews says about Jesus being a Son but still having to learn obedience through suffering. Thus the same letter later observes that those whom God loves he also chastises.

How respond to these people? Pray for them. There are

no techniques that can coerce them into openness. Only God can do it. Pray that they may learn quickly, in God's best way for them. But they will have to learn sometime, for the purposes of God will not be thwarted forever.

Chapter 5

THE COMMUNITY OF THE SPIRIT

God's Plan for Creation

In the letter to the Ephesians Paul describes the full scope of the purpose of God for the world as "gathering together all things in Christ." In speaking of this plan and how it is being carried out, he refers to the ascension of Jesus and to the day of Pentecost.

There is one body and one Spirit, just as you were called together in one hope which belongs to that call. . . . Grace was given to each of us according to the measure of Christ's gift. Therefore it is said, "When he ascended on high he led the capturers into captivity and he gave gifts to men." . . . He . . . ascended far above all the heavens that he might fill all things. And his gifts were that some should be apostles, some prophets, some evangelists, some pastors and teachers for the uniting together of the saints to carry out the works of service and to build up the body of Christ. [Eph. 4]

Paul says that it is God's intention to fill all things with Himself. In Christian thought God's purpose is almost always defined in reference to events in the life of Christ. Some concentrate on his ministry of teaching and say that the divine plan for men is for them to learn the proper way of living with their fellows in love and peace. Generally this is the position of liberal Protestantism. Some concentrate their theological attention on Good

Friday and the crucifixion. They say that God's plan is that men be freed from their sins through the death of Jesus. This is the position of evangelical Protestantism. Others dwell on the resurrection and imply that God's plan is that men be raised to a new and more spiritual existence. Generally this is the thrust of Eastern Orthodox theology. St. Paul, in this passage in Ephesians, calls our attention to Jesus' ascension and the coming of the Holy Spirit on Pentecost. Judging by these events, he says, God's purpose is to fill all things with Himself, to be all in all. The more man-centered ideas concerning it are means to this end. Jesus was a teacher and God wants men to learn from him, but this teaching is to help them participate in the over-all plan, which goes beyond just learning new things. Jesus died to redeem men, and God wants men relieved of the burden of sin, yet not as an end in itself but to free them to be parts of His larger purpose. God intends that men should be raised from the dead to live eternally—not for their own sake, but to share in the final time when He will be "all in all."

God's intention, then, is that all His creation shall be filled with His presence. How does He mean to accomplish this? In Ephesians Paul names one of the processes by which that purpose is being carried out. He says it is accomplished by giving "gifts" to men, and the gifts he lists are very similar to the spiritual gifts he speaks of to the Corinthians (prophecy, teachings, etc.). The function of these gifts is the same in both Ephesians and Corinthians: forming the believers into community. And the reason God wants people filled with His Spirit, the reason He wants His church built up as the full body of Christ, is because He wants us to share in His great purpose. When one becomes involved in the full life of the Spirit, one carries forth the purpose of God. In weighing the charismatic movement, one is not considering simply another conflicting group within the church. Indeed, one ought to take off his shoes, for one is on holy ground—looking at something that lies at the heart of

God's vision for His world. For the spiritual gifts and the Spirit-filled community that results from them are intimate parts of His work.

This is why, for Paul, there is a close relationship between the gifts of the Spirit and Christian community. All his references to spiritual gifts take place in the context of what he has to say about the church. And his metaphor of the church as a body is used primarily in connection with the discussion of spiritual gifts. Throughout, they are described as being "for the common good," or "that the church may be built up." In Ephesians the giving of the Spirit refers to the various offices in the church. The work of the Spirit is described as "uniting together" the saints into the body of Christ. The Spirit belongs basically to the community and not to the individual; it belongs to the individual only to the extent that he in turn belongs to the body.

The sectarian tradition imposed its congregational polity (which defines the church as a collection of individuals) on Paul's understanding of the spiritual gifts. Often the classical Pentecostals have implied that they are given primarily to individuals, and to the church only because it is an assembly of individuals. This is just the opposite of Paul's insistence that the Spirit belongs primarily to the body, which is not a mere collection of separate persons but the body of Christ.

This is also true of the fruits of the Spirit, which as listed in Galatians are all social—they are what makes for unity in the body. Paul defines them by contrast with what he calls the works of the flesh (cf. Gal. 5:16 ff.), which are primarily things that lead to schism in the body of Christ. He says that sectarianism and divisions disrupting the unity of the church are works of the flesh and can never be works of the Spirit. The purpose of the Spirit's sanctifying work is not to make you holier than your neighbor or more righteous than your friends. Rather it is to transform you into the kind of person who is able to live in community with your brothers and sisters. The gifts of the Spirit are its functional manifestation in the community; the fruits of the Spirit are its ethical manifestation.

The plan of God, then, culminates in the formation of Christian community. Paul implies in his letters to the Ephesians and Colossians that someday the church and all creation will be the Spirit-filled body of Christ. Even in our transitional state, the church is at once an instrument and a sign of the fulfillment of this plan. A sign because in the Spirit-filled community one gets a sense of what it will be like when all creation is itself a community filled with the Spirit of God. The existence of the church gives us a clue as to what it means to say that an organization can be filled with the Spirit. It, too, is an instrument, or may be. As more and more people are brought under the dominion of the Holy Spirit, God's purpose to fill all things with Himself is carried forth.

Since Christian community is crucial, it is important to know how it is understood in the New Testament. The Greek word *koinonia*—community—is the ordinary word for the most intimate relationship possible, including sexual union. When the Epistles come to describe the most basic experience of Christianity, they use that term. To be a Christian is to experience *koinonia*. In Romans, Paul says that the Gentiles have come into *koinonia* with the Holy Spirit (15:27). He tells the Corinthians that they have *koinonia* with the risen Lord. He describes man's relationship with God through the Spirit by this most intimate term: Christians live in *koinonia* with the Father, Son, and Holy Spirit. The first letter of John echoes the same theme: "What we have seen and heard, we announce to you, in order that you might have *koinonia* with us. Our *koinonia* is with the Father and with His son Jesus Christ." The two Petrine epistles reinforce this. The first proclaims that Christians live in *koinonia* with the glory of God Himself. Second Peter says that men participate in a *koinonia* with the very nature of God. The Epistles, then, with remarkable consistency describe man's experience of God in terms of the most intimate relationship possible. Through Christ, man lives in community with God. There are two other ways in which the term community is used in the New Testament, important for our purposes here. One is in describing the sacraments. In one of his best-known sacramental passages Paul writes, "The cup of blessing which we bless, is it not a *koinonia* in the blood of Christ; the bread which we break, is it not a *koinonia* in the body of Christ? For we who are many are a single body because of the single loaf, for all partake of that single loaf" (1 Cor. 10:16–17). Later he says that those who eat the sacrifice "have a *koinonia* with the altar." Since the term "body of Christ" refers both to the single but broken bread and the community composed of individual but unified members, Paul notes that the sacrament is another means of building the body. By using the same word, *koinonia*, to describe both the eucharistic bond between Christ and ourselves and the encounter with him and with each other in the church, he makes several points. He implies that participation in a charismatic community is not to lead us away from the sacraments. Just the opposite: it should lead us deeper into the sacramental life, for the sacraments are a *koinonia* and they build *koinonia*. The charismatic *koinonia* provides a communal context in which the sacramental *koinonia* can be lived to the fullest. Those Pentecostals who claim to be "full-gospel" but who emphasize the gifts more than either the sacraments or the church ignore the fact that the "full-gospel" experience of the gifts of the Spirit is in the context of the body of Christ—in the sense both of the sacraments and of the community.

Thus Catholics who worry that attending to spiritual gifts will undermine the sacramental life have little to fear. The gifts of the Spirit enrich it by building up the *koinonia* in which it can be most fully experienced. Exercise of spiritual gifts with increasing openness to the Lord often leads to a new appreciation of the sacraments. I once met a Protestant minister who, after being involved in the charismatic movement, began to attend regular weekday Communion services at an Episcopal church because his charismatic experience drew him to the sacraments. And I know evangelicals from a nonsacramental tradition who have found new significance in them through charismatic experience.

After the early controversy with the Montanists, mentioned earlier, a gradual division developed in the church between the charismatic ministry and the sacramental ministry. But in the New Testament church no such division existed. The first epistle to Timothy contains two references which combine Timothy's sacramental ordination with the charismatic ministry. In 1:18, "I commit this charge to you, my child Timothy, according to the preceding prophecies given to you, that by them you might fight the good fight," and in 4:14, "Do not neglect the charism [i.e., "spiritual gift"] which was given you through prophecy and the laying on of hands by the elders." Obviously Timothy's service of ordination included the exercise of spiritual gifts. In First Corinthians, Paul is giving instructions about "assembling together" for community meetings. He begins by instructing them in the importance of unity (11:17 ff.), then about the importance of the Eucharist (11:23 ff.). And then, without a break, he begins to instruct them as to spiritual gifts (12:1 ff.). All this is under the general rubric of how to do business in the assembly. Obviously, the community meetings included both the Eucharist and charismatic gifts as one whole. This is reinforced in an interesting verse in chapter 14 where Paul says, "If you bless [the same word he used in 10:16 to refer to the bread and wine] in the Spirit, how can the uninstructed say the 'amen' to your Eucharist since he doesn't know what you've said. You may have made Eucharist well, but he is not edified" (14:16–17). These verses may refer to a Corinthian practice of saying the Eucharist in tongues!

In the New Testament, then, there is no opposition or friction between the sacramental and the charismatic life. Both are elements of one life in the body of Christ. The modern charismatic movement says that the time for old polemics is past. Churches which claim to be "full-gospel," in which the sacramental life has atrophied, and those that cling to the sacraments while decrying the exercise of spiritual gifts as fanatical, are both sectarian. They have both lost touch with the full life. One group may see the sacraments only in terms of personal piety or as an opportunity to put on extravagant display; the other may understand spiritual gifts in the same way. They have alike lost sight of Paul's concern that both sacraments and *charismata* be understood in terms of building up the full life of body of Christ. In some classical and neo-Pentecostal churches as well as in the Catholic charismatic movement, that life is being restored as Christians seek to combine again the sacramental *koinonia* and the charismatic *koinonia* in a total life in Christian community.

The other way, important here, in which the word *koinonia* is used in the New Testament is to describe Christians' relations to one another. Paul often speaks of others as those who have *koinonia* with him in the gospel. The phrase is usually rendered "to be partners" with him, that is, to have a "part" with him, to "participate" with him in the gospel. The same single word is used to describe our relationship with God, through the Spirit and the sacraments, and with one another in the church. This means that our relation to our brothers and sisters in Christ is to be as intimate as our relationship with Christ himself as he dwells within us through Spirit and sacrament. And this is to be as close as our most intimate human friendship! Think about that for a while.

This is what Christian community means. Look around at the churches you have known. The relation of Christians is to be as deep and pervasive as man's most profound religious experience: the experience of community or communion (the same word in Greek) with God! And man's relation to God is to be as deep and intimate as the closest human relation. This is the standard by which religious experience is to be judged: Does it produce an ever more intimate walk with God and an equally close community among people?

The New Testament, then, chooses the most intimate term possible in describing the essence and full range of Christian experience. To be a Christian is to experience *koinonia*—to live in *koinonia* with God and with one's brothers and sisters and to look forward to that day when all men and all creation will be a *koinonia* with each other and with God, who will be "all in all."

Building the Body

Several practical things follow as to how community is formed. First of all, it is intimate sharing and involvement that in fact makes a group a community—not physical or geographical closeness. Just gathering people together in one place does not make a community. This applies both to members of religious orders and to people interested in religious communities or secular communes. I have known several groups of college students who have rented houses or apartments together. They are all students, with common inclinations and ideologies; they live under the same roof, maybe in the same bed; they take their meals together. This seduces them into thinking they have a community, but it soon becomes apparent that they do not. Personal problems spread poison in the body politic. Some hold back as much as they contribute (remember Ananias and Sapphira). Differences over politics or morality become schisms in the house. Because there is little authority, the dirty jobs gradually stop getting done. Soon members begin to drop away.

Just living together—eating and sleeping together, sharing

common interests—will not even begin to form community. The same is true of marriages. Common interests and mutual attraction are not enough to build a marriage. How many marriages have gone sour because no real community can be built on these feeble foundations! For it demands sharing, actually participating in each other's lives. Early Christians were a community, not because they shared a common interest in Jesus, but because they actually participated through the Spirit in his life.

Thus community is not an institutional structure. It is a "style" of Christian living. Since it is not synonymous with physical proximity, *koinonia* does not demand that people live under the same roof. It does not demand that they pool their incomes, for the spiritual reality cannot be identified with any human economic arrangement. It does not require them to break up into small groups; Christian community is built by the Spirit and not by human techniques of group psychology. Some people get so hung up on institutional arrangements that they completely lose sight of the fact that *koinonia* is first a reality of the Spirit and only then a sociological structure.

I have seen deep Christian community in small households where people do all live under one roof; I have visited groups living in one house where sullen hostility and passive resignation reign supreme. I have been a member of a community of six hundred which only met together once a week, where the sense of *koinonia* was a wonder to behold—and have seen small groups of ten or twelve from whom the real experience was as far as the east is from the west. Thus *koinonia* cannot be identified with any institutional form. How it is expressed institutionally (small groups or large, households or prayer communities) each group must decide for itself as the Spirit leads. Each must begin from the experience of *koinonia* itself and let the structure take shape out of it. To proceed from a fixed idea of structure is to build only a hollow shell. This is not to say that

certain kinds of structure will not help—they certainly will.*
But they must grow organically out of the primary experience
of *koinonia.*

The next practical thing that follows from a New Testament
understanding of the subject is that Christian communities are
not the same as prayer meetings. They will certainly hold meetings for prayer, but I would prefer to call them prayer communities. Why this rather artificial distinction? By a prayer
meeting one tends to mean a gathering where people come
primarily to have their own needs met. They come mainly to
get a spiritual blessing for themselves, doing collectively what
each of them would do at home in their private prayers. There
is nothing necessarily wrong with this, but it does not build
community. One comes to a "prayer meeting" concerned about
the relation of one's soul to God. In a prayer community people
gather not only to fulfill their own needs but also to build up the
body of Christ. They come to share and minister to one another,
and to allow the community to minister to them, and to grow
in concrete love for each other. Any blessing one receives is a
product of the whole spiritual experience of the community
and not a narrow personal aim.

Many times I have people ask me, "Why does our prayer
group stay so small? Why does it just limp along?" I have seen
tiny prayer groups of five or six faithful souls just struggling
along. Often the reason these groups do not grow to communities of several hundred is because they are not communities at
all but mere collections of individuals doing together what each
does in private anyway. Since they do not form community,
they are not ready to deal with several hundred, and the Lord
does not send them greater numbers. Sometimes these groups
gradually fade away—not because there is not need for prayer

---

*For a practical discussion of building community see Stephen Clark, *Build-
ing Christian Communities* (Notre Dame, Ind.: Ave Maria Press, 1972).

—far from it—but because their members do not understand the Lord's will. The Lord wants his body built up: that is, He wants people to grow in love and service to Him and each other —the formation of real Christian community. If prayer groups do not understand this, they will not grow. They may continue to serve a specific function in a parish, meeting the private needs of members; but they will not be playing their full role in the plan of God, which is to have the body of Christ formed in its fullness, wholly ready for service.

The same is true of Pentecostal groups who meet only to glory in spiritual gifts. That is glorying in the flesh, no matter how impressive the gifts may appear. I do not think what the Lord wants is a lot of little prayer groups or even a lot of large charismatic assemblies. Remember the prophecy given to David Du Plessis. What the Lord wants is His whole body, His whole church renewed as the body of Christ. Small charismatic meetings and large charismatic assemblies may be transitional instruments to that end, but the goal of Pentecostal churches and charismatic communities alike ought to be to put themselves out of business, pointing to the time when all churches will be thus revitalized and the spiritual gifts incorporated into their full life. This will never happen if the Lord has only inward-looking prayer meetings to work with; it can only come about if His people are radically open to the call of His Spirit.

In light of this, there is another implication in the New Testament idea of community. It concerns those I call "prayer-meeting hoppers." Sometimes you meet people who move from group to group, going to another meeting almost every night of the week. They belong to no single community but take what suits them from everyone else's meetings, never under the discipline of any community, never allowing any community to form and mold them. They never *build* community because they never stay in any one place long enough. There is nothing wrong with visiting various groups, so long as you are a member of one group where you are contributing to the building up of true community. If you have this concern, then find a group where you feel the Lord wants you and stay there! When times of trouble come to it, as they will to any community, then don't go looking for greener pastures but "hang in there" so that it can be the body of Christ to you. If the group starts to grow, be very careful if you feel the Lord is calling you to go off and start another group of your own. Nine times out of ten He probably is not, for I do not think the Lord wants a lot of struggling little groups; he wants the full body of Christ built up.

The final practical implication of the New Testament understanding of *koinonia* is that community is formed by the Spirit, not by the law. The building is something God does, not we ourselves. We are all concerned about what we can do, how we can get involved, finding the right technique and getting organized. This is the mark of Cain upon our foreheads, the sign of the activistic and technique-minded society in which we live. There *are no techniques* for building Christian community. There are mistakes one can look out for, and ground that can be spaded up so that the seed of God's word can take root more easily, but these will not guarantee the result. There is no sure-fire, humanly conceived way to build community, for God, not man, is the master builder.

I am sure this book would be a lot more popular if I could write, "Follow these five easy (or even difficult) steps, and you'll have a brand new Christian community just waiting for you." This is what our pride wants and what the world wants from us: a technique, a pat solution that will work infallibly like a machine. That would indeed feed our self-importance, for then we could say, "Look what I'm doing! I'm building Christian community!" We would want credit for it, and the credit would puff us up until we ceased to look at God and depend upon Him and began to look more and more at ourselves. But there is only one way in which the Spirit is released, only one way in which the plan of God is carried out, and that is through surrender and humility, through openness and responsiveness.

The primary way by which Christian community is built, is
—oddly enough—by men and women waiting humbly on the
Lord until nothing happens. They get discouraged. And they
get depressed. And they get impatient. And finally they either
go away in anger or truly open themselves to His will and
accept the fact that He is going to do things His own way and
His own good time. And then they begin to praise and thank
Him for what they had earlier thought of as His terrible slow-
ness and hardness of heart toward them. Then their wills are
cracked, and His will can be done through them; then they are
broken open and can be filled. They are supple enough in the
Spirit to allow Him to work.

In the New Testament, the law is what lays demands upon us.
Much as we may chafe under them, secretly we like them. For
when we fulfill what is required we can take pride in what we
have done, and thus the law saves us from what we fear most:
the breaking of pride and the crushing of the ego. Now, the
gospel frees us from the law with its endless demands. But it is
a paradoxical freedom, for it prepares us for a far more terrible
obligation, that of being responsive to the Spirit. On man's side,
the process by which the Spirit is released and gifts exercised
is the same as that by which community is formed—a humble
openness to the will of God. That is why there is such a close
connection between the release of the Spirit and the building
of community. Just as there are no techniques for forming
Christian community, so exercise of the *charismata* is in fact the
opposite of a technique; it is the paradoxical undermining of all
technique, for it is the manifestation of a radical willingness to
renounce the will and to be responsive to the Spirit.

Maturity and Community

We have seen why it is theologically important that Christian
community be formed as one of the major instruments of God.

I want to say a few words about another phase of this: why community is necessary for the individual to grow in the Spirit. For here is where one is formed into a spiritual person. There are several ways in which a developed, Spirit-filled Christian community will help to do this.

1. By making one more sensitive to the Spirit. I have mentioned how our culture desensitizes us to anything outside our own circle of egoism: by ideologies which inflate our pride, telling us that self-aggrandizement comes first; by overwhelming our powers of concern with more human suffering than we can empathize with; and by encasing us in comfort until we cannot break out of the realm of self-concern. To the extent that we are incapable of responding to the interests of others and are insensitive to the claims of those outside our immediate circle, to that extent we cannot eagerly respond to God or be open to His Spirit. A willingness (though we may often fail at it) to be responsive to God even in the midst of suffering, and to be open to Him even to the point of exercising the spiritual gifts, proves our readiness to overcome this desensitizing and break into a fuller life in the Spirit.

A community in which the presence of the Spirit of God is readily apparent helps to resensitize us to that presence. If one is constantly exposed to the presence and power of God until one cannot deny it, one is made much more aware of that presence in ordinary life. I was once involved in a multimedia, hard-rock worship service on a college campus. It was one of my first exposures to this style of worship and entertainment, and I asked the group why they felt such loud, bombastic techniques were necessary. They replied that people were bored and distracted with more modulated music and that this high-powered material was the only way to rivet their attention and, as they put it, "get through to the kids"—an interesting phrase, implying that there is some barrier in the audience. (Get through *what* in order to reach them?) Right after this I went on a short retreat with a group of friends to a cabin in the woods of Minnesota. I was used to the woods, being an inveterate hiker and camper, but many of those present had spent little time outdoors. Soon I began to pick up the usual sounds: a bird's frail chirping, the wind blowing against the leaves, a squirrel running through the grass. Those who had rarely heard them did not readily notice these small noises, but being directed learned to listen for them, and everyone eventually became aware of the sounds of the woods. From this I concluded that it is not always necessary to bombard people. One can become sensitive to even the gentlest experience (like wind upon leaves) if one is made aware of it and shown how to listen for it and attend to it.

This is what a Spirit-filled community does. It provides an experience of the presence of God. The community is a place where the Spirit is *really* present—that is, in such a way that even many who come dead set against the idea find that they really do have the experience in unmistakable terms. Besides making this possible, the community helps to focus on it. The spiritual gifts of edification, such as prophecy, discernment, or teaching, are aids in recognizing the movement of the Spirit. If it is really guiding the community, one will develop a sense of what that guidance is like and begin to recognize it in one's own life. Thus the first way the community forms one into a spiritual person is by making possible direct experience of the Spirit and sensitizing one to it.

2. A second way the community forms the spiritual person is through teaching. In Acts 2:42 it is said that the early converts "gave themselves to the apostles' teaching and the *koinonia* and the breaking of the bread." All three go together in Christian experience. Without the spirit-filled *koinonia*, Christian teaching becomes arid, abstract intellectualism. Without teaching, the *koinonia* can easily go off into sectarianism and heresy. When I have come across prayer groups and communities with

problems, the reason is more often than not a lack of sound teaching. Perhaps people have not understood the purpose of the spiritual gifts or what to do with them. They have tremendous power released into their lives but no idea how to direct it. Or they do not quite know how to conduct themselves at prayer meetings. So many difficulties that Pentecostals have run into might have been avoided or softened had there been better teaching. For a community to grow in the Spirit there must be common teaching about the baptism in the Spirit and the nature and purpose of spiritual gifts. It is vital that people not only have the same experience but also understand it in the same way. Only then can experience of the Spirit unify God's people.

Throughout the New Testament there is a balance. Jesus says that those who worship the Father must worship Him in spirit and in truth. I always wondered what that meant, but since becoming involved in the charismatic movement I think I know. There must be a balance between spirit and truth. Many groups have the truth of Christianity, but devoid of any Spirit it hangs over their heads like a weight almost too heavy to carry. Others have lots of Spirit but very little truth. They go off on tangents, get lost in back eddies of spirituality, and may even depart from Christianity without knowing it. The groups that have lots of Spirit but little truth are no better off than those with only the shell of doctrine to protect them. Neither can lead one into the Kingdom of God. Thus teaching is one of the primary means by which one grows in the Spirit. Paul constantly emphasizes that the church must be "edified" and condemns those who pursue false doctrine.

3. The ministries of counseling and healing. Christian community enables brothers and sisters to minister to one another and fulfill the New Testament injunction to "bear one another's burdens." We all need this from time to time. We all have areas in our lives which are not the way the Lord wants them to be.

As one grows in the Spirit, more and more of these areas are turned up. When those of us who were going to have some responsibility for overseeing the life of the community in St. Paul began to meet together, we found that we had to spend the first several months of our meetings ministering to one another. It was not a question of mental health; no one there had any abnormal psychological difficulties. But before we could minister to the whole community we had to first learn to serve each other. The Lord made it very clear that he wanted each of us to submit to the rest. It is vital that we serve one another. Not because some "need" it more than others, but because that is the way the body of Christ is built up. No one should ask anyone to come to him or her for counseling or prayer or any ministry who is not also being ministered to by someone else. No one can minister in a Christian community who is not also being ministered to. One of the most important ways in which community is formed and maintained is by people submitting themselves to each other and bearing one another's burdens, as the scripture puts it.

This is where Paul's image is so instructive. Everyone is a part of the body. It is not all one limb; it cannot be all hands or feet or eyes or ears. No one person has all the gifts of the Spirit, but in a community of wide range, those with certain gifts can help those who need them, receiving in turn help from others who have what they themselves lack. This is why so many small groups never develop into the full body of Christ. Few groups of only five or six have all the gifts of the Spirit. Maybe one or two will have gifts of healing, so that the group concentrates on healing but does not move as the Lord intends because there is no leadership. Or perhaps there is one strong leader and everyone rallies around him, but there is no teaching. Or a lot of tongues, but few of the gifts of edification. But in a full Christian community, all these gifts are present and can find their place. Paul says that "to each is given a spiritual gift for the common good." If there are many members, then there are many gifts and the group will not get lopsided in the direction of healing or teaching or speaking in tongues, and thus all can minister to one another.

Everyone runs across problems in trying to live a deeper life in the Spirit. One uncovers certain blocks to the Spirit's flow—certain "hang-ups," certain questions and areas of confusion. If one is to grow, one needs to be a member of a community where one can be ministered to when these arise. Some people, when things take a turn downward, withdraw. Don't! Many problems people have in living the Christian life come from attempting to live it individually. As difficulties increase they withdraw from their brothers and sisters, and that makes the problems even worse. Christians are meant to be members of a body; they ought not leave it when they need it most. In times of tension, strain, or struggle the Lord is often calling on one to grow up a bit, and the community is a major means or channel of that growth. If one withdraws, growth will be stunted.

Thus it is important that one be open to ministry. Some say, "I want to serve and help others," but do not seem to contribute to community. Why? Usually because they are not open to others ministering to *them*. They use their concern for others as a defense to keep others from getting to know them better. But it is my weakness that gives you a chance to minister to me, and it is your difficulties that give me a chance to minister to you, and this is one way community is formed. The body is built up by the various ministries of the Spirit working together, knitting together strength to weakness, ministry to need. A Christian should not refuse to submit to the community or to be open to the body of Christ, for only thus can he be built into it and helped when in need, and so be formed into a spiritual person.

4. The final formative function of the community is the support it gives in living the life of the Spirit. There are clearly

several areas of conflict between our culture and that life. We find ourselves in an age of unprecedented materialism, where only outward signs of success are really approved. There is a total reliance on man's will; it is a culture of pride and self-assertion. As we saw above, this is in itself desensitizing and obscures our awareness of others and of God. Religion is only supported in our society to the extent that it buttresses "social values." One will get little support for living the life of the Spirit.

But the *koinonia* gives the encouragement and sustenance that is needed. In Minnesota it was very clear that those who became a part of the community, who made friends there and participated in it, were the ones who grew in the Spirit. I can see the same thing happening in smaller communities. Those who are deeply involved grow by leaps and bounds. Those who come occasionally or do not participate spiritually stagnate. The Lord is constantly calling Christians to a deeper life with Him, and this means a deeper life in His body.

The fact that our culture—the values of its institutions, the imagery of its mass media, the language of its social commerce —will supply little nourishment or acceptance of the spiritual life confronts us with three options: One is that of withdrawing from the world, condemning it as godless and immoral. This does not accord well with Christian theology, which names Jesus the Lord of the world and calls upon men to proclaim His lordship over this actual scene in which we live and work and vote and suffer and die. It does not ask us to predate the final Kingdom by setting up utopian cells separate from the world. Another possibility is to assimilate to the culture and give up many of the values of the gospel. No one who seriously wants to grow in the Spirit can entertain it. The final option is to live in tension with one's society. This is the hardest of all but seems to accord best with the gospel injunction to live out the lordship of Christ over the world. Jesus himself marked out this choice when he said we must be in the world but not of it. The gospel nowhere suggests withdrawing from the world (Paul explicitly forbids it in 1 Cor. 5:10), but does enjoin not being "of" it.

To those who take the first, sectarian option the function of the church is to provide a haven from the world—"an island of holiness in a sea of sin" as one sixteenth-century Anabaptist leader put it. For those who pursue the second choice, on the other hand, the church is an unnecessary encumbrance, a residual social institution to be dismantled as quickly as possible. But for those who follow the third possibility, the church must be the full body of Christ, from which they can obtain the teaching and ministry and support necessary to live in the world without being swamped by it. Many who try to carry on a full Christian life apart from a rounded Christian community find themselves dragged down by the pressures of living, or subject to roller-coaster mood swings, or frustrated by their lack of impact on the society they seek to serve. Being members of a full community in Christ would give them the support to withstand these pressures—would stabilize their Christian lives and help them realize that no one individual is supposed to change the world. For the body of Christ rather than isolated individuals is the instrument through which God works on earth.

Therefore, if one seeks a deeper life in the Spirit, one must know that this can take place best in the context of a group of people who come together in whatever way to worship the Lord and grow in His love. The goal of the Spirit's work is to form community, and if this does not happen, the work is frustrated and the instruments of God blunted. The development of a person in the Spirit is linked both to growth within community and to the growth of the community to which one belongs. Very rarely can individuals mature faster than the body of which they are members. One will mature as one's community grows. I have seen so many instances in which people new in the Spirit matured rapidly because they became part of a mature community, and so many others in which those who began well floundered because their community floundered. It is God's will that Christians be members one of another, that they bear one anothers' burdens, and share the joys and sorrows of a common life and so fulfill the call of Christ.

Q. Have you any comments to make about the number of communities that have arisen in the last few years? Is there something in these movements for us in the church to think about?

A. Yes. There is clearly a renewed interest in community both in religious groups and in secular communes. I think the church must take a close look at these movements. It should examine its own life in light of the importance of life in community. The Christian insight into the nature of community has a lot to contribute to the general interest. I am currently doing some writing on the relation of these movements to the church: what the church should learn from them, what it should watch out for in them, and what its unique contribution might be. The cultural and political questions involved in forming community in this society are crucial, but obviously that's a whole other topic.

Q. So often, in the history of the church and the tension between culture and community, a stress on the latter has led to sectarianism—setting up a rigid moral code prohibiting dancing, drinking, smoking, and cutting a person off from the world. In the Pentecostal movement you frequently have this tendency towards sectarianism and perfectionism (a move to erase all evil in the community). Are you aware enough of these dangers in what you have proposed?

A. I don't know. I am certainly aware of them in my own mind. I have tried to say as clearly as possible that the Christian is not to withdraw from the world, or assimilate to it, but to live in tension with it. Here an emphasis on community is not a utopian denial of the world but a turning to the only agency that can enable one actually to live in this tension and not "cop out" by withdrawal or assimilation. As for rigid moralism and perfectionism, as a professor of American religious history I cannot resist pointing out that this is an almost uniquely American problem because of the impact of the sectarian, pietistic, perfectionistic ethos on all our institutions, especially the churches. The charismatic movement which came most directly out of that ethos (the classical Pentecostals) exemplifies it to an extreme. But when the movement arises in churches which have a fuller contact with the great historic traditions of Christianity beyond American evangelicalism, it does not fall prey to excessive moralism and sectarianism. In the Catholic, Anglican, Lutheran, and some Reformed churches in this country—to say nothing of the charismatic movement abroad—these problems exist to a far lesser extent. The only real answer is the answer to sectarianism in general: an emphasis on and appreciation of the great historic traditions of Christian life and thought.

Q. In any one of these charismatic communities is there likely to be a denominational spread or do they tend to be pretty much of one denomination?

A. Again, this is a sociological question for which I don't have the data. My experience would be that there are two kinds of charismatic assemblies. One could be called Catholic. It is not all Roman Catholic, but generally its members come from "Catholic" or "high-church" traditions—Roman, Anglican, Lutheran, and some Reformed—which emphasize the continuity of the church and the sacramental life. The second might be called evangelical. Its members are not all classical Pentecostals but come from Methodist, Baptist, and other evangelical denominations. Many Catholic charismatic groups are not all Roman Catholic, many are about half-and-half. But they generally draw their non-Roman membership from other high-church traditions. The same is true with "evangelical" groups; members of some denominations tend to go to groups with an evangelical ethos. In these two kinds of groups there is denominational spread within those limits. Few groups have only one church represented, and many have representatives from both Catholic and evangelical churches as I have defined them. But in general these two kinds of groups may be distinguished. As the ecumenical aspect of the charismatic movement continues, this may change.

Q. When you speak about building the body of Christ I find myself giving intellectual assent to what you say, but only partially. Even the church is only a part-time community for me. I belong to so many other things. There is merely token continuity between them.

A. This is a fine comment—thank-you. It raises a very crucial question. The sectarian says that the church is the only community. Most of us live in a plurality of communities. For many of us our family is the primary one (although there may be another sense in which the body of Christ is the primary community, but that is to raise the question of the place of families in Christian community—a topic beyond our scope here). This is the frustrating thing about working with college students, most of whom have only a single commitment and community—their studies and their peer group—and find it hard to understand the problems of a world where people live with many commitments and communities and responsibilities. This may be why the early strong Catholic charismatic communities were found on college campuses, among unmarried students who were used to having only one commitment and community. Some of their teaching was not completely useful in forming community among older people who already had families and responsible jobs in the world.

Most of us live in a plurality of communities. I don't think we should try to see one community as primary, or even one community (even the church) as more related to Christ. Rather I think we must struggle to see Jesus as equally the Lord of all communities in which we live: the family, the church, the job, the club, and so on. It is not our task to set the church over against the shop or the home, as though the church *qua* institution were more important than the institutions of family, job, or the civil order. Rather we must proclaim the lordship of Jesus Christ equally over all institutions and communities. The importance of the church is not that it is the only community where Christ is Lord. That is a sectarian truncating of the gospel. It may very well be the only community where Jesus is now acknowledged as Lord, but he is still Lord over the state and business, the trade union and the classroom. The importance of the church is that it is the community which enables us to proclaim and live out the lordship of Christ over all the communities in which we live. This may be the only continuity we can find in them—that they all stand under the lordship of Christ and call upon us to live out that lordship in their context.

Chapter 6

THE RELEASE OF THE SPIRIT

Can Church Renewal Renew the Church?

I come finally to the most important and difficult aspect of our topic: the renewal of the church. We have seen all along that this is the purpose of the charismatic movement. If it cannot strengthen and revitalize the church, then it will not have succeeded regardless of how many brilliant religious experiences or flashy miracles it produces. The goal of the Pentecostal movement should be to put itself out of business. Ultimately it should not produce separate Pentecostal groups, but rather a renewed church in which the charismatic experience is readily incorporated. The Lord loves His church and has promised to be with it, and nothing Pentecostals do should give the impression that He has any intention of forsaking it.

There are two reasons why this is a most difficult subject. First, because it puts us on the front line of the charismatic movement. It brings up problems which the movement is just now beginning to face and about which it has not yet clearly seen the leading of the Lord. What has been so far said is grounded in a great deal of experience and reflection, ripened over time. The movement has had time to mature in the understanding of spiritual gifts; it has had time to gain experience and wisdom in the building of Christian community. But it is only just beginning to confront the nitty-gritty problems of church renewal, and has not really had time as yet to experience, discern, and reflect. There are therefore bound to be mistakes—experiments that fail because they are not quite what the Lord wants. Yet how else do we learn but a little at a time?

The second difficulty in approaching this topic lies in the fact that it is hard to discuss without appearing to be uncharitably critical. Whenever one speaks of renewal, there is an implication of criticism. To say the church stands in need of it suggests that there is something wrong, and those who love the church immediately become defensive. Moreover, to speak of a need for charismatic renewal in particular implies that other phases and vehicles of vitalization have not worked. One is on thin ice when one judges, for the Lord has said, "Beware, the judgment you shall pass will be the judgment you will receive." The problem is one of love. Before I wrote this I spent a lot of time in prayer that it might be said in love for the church and the people of God. Paul says that we must "speak the truth in love." It would not be loving *not* to speak the truth in the frankest way, but it would not be Christian to speak out of hostility or bitterness, with an intention—however unconscious—to destroy rather than to build up.

This is an exciting time to be involved in church renewal, but we pay a price for it. There is a heavy toll in anxiety because the future is not clear; in frustration when things move too fast or too slow; in confusion over the clash of ideas and programs. It is well to recall that we must often walk by faith and not by sight, for we live "between the times"—perhaps the most important thing to keep in mind when discussing church renewal today. For the old is passing away, but the new has not yet appeared. This means we cannot predict. I do not write as a prophet; I cannot tell you what the church will look like in twenty years. At best, all I can describe are a few minor steps which might be taken at present, and I cannot foresee exactly what effect they will have in the future.

Living between the times also means that no structures we

establish can be permanent. None of the practical forms I discuss should be seen as abiding institutions. They are not; they
are stages along the way which should be abandoned as soon as
their usefulness to God's purposes is finished. Living in such a
transitional period with a radical openness to God's Spirit
means being ever on guard against allowing forms and structures and programs to fossilize, become bureaucratic, and develop a life of their own instead of service to a greater end, so
that they refuse humbly to disband when they are no longer of
use to that goal. I suspect that the present structures of the
charismatic movement are to the renewed church as scaffolding is to a building. One must erect the scaffolding, so that the
building can be built. But you cannot stop there and claim that
you have now put up the building. And when the latter is
indeed completed, it is important that the scaffolding should be
dismantled and fall away, for its purpose has been served, and
to leave it in place will obscure and hide rather than support the
building.

All that has been said about the renewal of the individual
applies as strongly to the renewal of the church. Let us recall
briefly that (1) the charismatic movement is a release of the
Spirit, and (2) the Spirit cannot be released by techniques but
only by humble openness and responsiveness. The first principle effectively denies the idea that before the baptism in the
Spirit the Christian is devoid of the Spirit or that it is only with
the Pentecostal movement that the Spirit enters the church.
Charismatic renewal of the church means that the Spirit at the
heart of the church is released with new and immediate power
into its life. Pentecostals who attack the church with the in-
nuendo that it lacks the Spirit do nothing to build it up. Indeed,
they may tear it down. If they are to call themselves the ser-
vants of Christ, then they must serve his body and use their
spiritual wisdom to guide the churches in releasing the Spirit
that pulses in their heart.

We have noted that Pentecost is often called the birthday of the church. This is no mere pious rhetoric; it is a fact that must be faced. If the church was born of the Spirit it must be renewed by the same great power. Renewal of the individual involves a deepening in the Spirit; the same is true of the church, whose life cannot be revitalized apart from that Spirit which was the source of it. The purpose of spiritual gifts is to release the Spirit not only into the life of the individual but also into the life of the body of Christ.

Implicit in the charismatic movement's work of renewal is the fact that any attempt to restore vitality to the church by tinkering with the ecclesiastical furniture, or redrawing its bureaucratic blueprint, without first experiencing a deeper life in the Spirit, is not only misguided, it is a sin. Whoever does this is trying to achieve by human effort what only the Spirit of God can do. Without a rebirth of the Spirit all plans for renewal—whether by social reform, sensitivity training, educational technique, or the like—will fail and become counterproductive. The fact is that the church lives by the Spirit, and in the Spirit is its only possibility of genuine renewal.

At issue is the theological doctrine of the church. If it is really the body of Christ, then we cannot understand it primarily by means of categories drawn from our own human institutions or clubs. The church is not primarily a sociological institution which has arisen partly by accident, or history, or because of social conditions, or through human decision, although God has worked through all of these to bring it into being. The church arose primarily by divine call. No one was asked whether he needed or wanted it; no one was surveyed to see if it was feasible or not. It arose out of God's free and sovereign act of pouring out His Spirit upon His children.

Two important things follow from this. First, we cannot take with ultimate seriousness those social-scientific studies of the church and their criticisms of it which are based on the assumption that it is simply a social institution to be understood on a

par with other institutions. We must listen to thoughtful analyses of this sort, but we cannot base our plans for renewal on
them. To the extent that the church is in the world, such criticism must be taken seriously. But what defines it and gives it its
true shape and substance and mission cannot be arrived at by
the use of categories drawn from a generalized study of human
institutions.

Second, since this is so, plans for renewal or for ecumenical
relations which are simply bureaucratic reshuffling will not
touch the essence of the church either in its unity or disunity.
Since man did not create it, he does not control it. It is not his
to do with as he pleases. He cannot, at his whim, turn it into a
sensitivity session, an educational institution, or a community
agency. The fact is, it does not exist to serve itself as an institution or some abstraction such as "Christian values"; it exists to
serve its concrete and living Lord.

Thus renewal for the church, as for the individual, must begin
with a deeper release of the Spirit that lives within it. Any plans
for renewal which do not begin here, no matter how beautiful
or sound in appearance, are bound to fail. If the church is first
the body of Christ, then all planning for renewal must reflect
this rather than any external form. Or, stated inversely, all its
visible social forms must *express* rather than determine the
essence of the church as the body of Christ; its structures must
grow out of the life of the body. This means that renewal must
begin with that life, which is primary, and not its form, which
is derivative.

This brings us to another point which is the same for the
church as for the individual: that life in the Spirit is released and
deepened not by techniques but by a humble openness to the
Lord. It is in this perspective, I think, that we must view the
various modern movements for church renewal. As a
seminarian and priest, I have been involved in most of them—
renewal through the social apostolate, through the liturgy,

through methods of group psychology, and so on. Here I must say honestly and with great sorrow that all of them have failed to renew the church as the body of Christ. I am not knocking them; they are all good things and I support them all. And each has produced great good in its own sphere, there is no denying that. But they were asked to do a job that was not theirs. Thus none of them, or all of them together, could renew the church as the body of Christ. Rather, each renewal movement has touched only a small fraction or strand of it. Each so-called revival of Christianity has revived less and less of it. These movements have produced in the church a welter of small groups, each doing its own thing, each competing for the time and resources of the church. They have fragmented rather than renewed it.

Why is this so? Let me take two examples from my own experience. The first concerns the church's social apostolate or mission. Let me be very clear about this, beyond any misunderstanding. The church *must* involve itself in the great social-political crises of the day. It calls Jesus Lord—this means that He is Lord of all the earth, and that His will of justice and mercy and love extends to the real world in which men work, vote, and carry on their commerce. It is the criterion by which this world will be judged on the Last Day. To refuse to struggle with turbulent contemporary issues—to run from them into hot-houses of piety—is to deny the most fundamental Christian truth and indeed the very lordship of Christ.

But when the church in the present day began to take its social apostolate seriously, it did so from the top down. Church bureaus issued official pronouncements. In their public office, church leaders engaged in private politics. There was no attempt to lead the church as a whole to an understanding of how these matters flow naturally out of the gospel. A social mission of some kind arises inevitably out of the Christian life, yet no attempt was made to convince laymen of this or to renew that basic Christian experience out of which a keen sense of the church's mission could grow. Rather, everything was done structurally. Committees were established, studies made, and church forms utilized for these ends. Many did not understand such programs, for they did not arise naturally out of a new spirit of mission. Nor, in fact, have they renewed the church—they did not touch the essence of its life, they only divided it.

The same is true of liturgical renewal. In every instance I know of (in my very limited experience), where there has been opposition to new forms of liturgy, people have felt that something is being forced on them. The reason they feel this way may not be because the pastor has been heavy-handed, but because they perceive the new liturgical experience itself as something forced. The revised liturgy attempts to achieve at least two things: an increased sense of celebration and greater lay participation. But many people do not have a larger sense of Christian joy and therefore regard the emphasis on celebration as an imposition. Many do not feel a vital renewal of their call as the people of God; thus the demand to participate more fully in its corporate life seems foreign. To attempt to renew the liturgical forms without first renewing the life of the people which gives rise to these forms is like producing new wineskins without the new wine to pour into them.

A friend of mine once served on a liturgical commission. She is a sensitive and astute laywoman. The commission sampled the greatest variety of possible liturgical diet, and she told me that after a while she noticed that some could enter into the experience of worship and some could not. Those who were capable of worship were able to find this experience in a Latin Mass or a jazz and dance celebration. Those who did not know how to worship at first blamed the outdated liturgical structures, but it soon became apparent that however radically they were changed, these people could not really pray. Soon the liturgy became for them a celebration of liturgical experimentation rather than any kind of celebration of the presence of God. Neither my friend nor I drew the most conservative possible conclusion from this story: that liturgy need never be revised. But it does show that attempts to revitalize forms of worship without first renewing the inner life and experiences out of which worship comes are doomed.

We need new forms of social apostolate, of liturgy, of personal relations within the body of Christ; but first we need a new life in the body of Christ to give rise to these forms. Let me illustrate with the same two areas. People who come into the charismatic movement have no greater sense of mission than average churchmen. But after being in the community in St. Paul for a while, one group became very interested in prisons and began to visit them and be concerned about the fate of society's outcasts. Another did the same for old people. Many tried to help young drug addicts. Some who had previously sneered at kids with long hair opened their homes to young refugees. Some worked with runaways. Yet no leader in the community ever spoke about the mission to the world; no one had preached that aging, prisons, and drugs were major issues in society with which the church must be involved. The deeper sense of mission arose naturally out of a deeper experience of the Christian life. And their mission in turn made possible a deeper personal growth in the Spirit. Thus there must be a renewal of the fruits of the Spirit in the social sphere, but these fruits can only grow out of a renewal by the Spirit and not out of external exhortations to increased activity.

Or again: the various experiences which liturgical renewal was supposed to induce—celebration, participation, and fellowship—happened naturally in the community, and the liturgy was returned to its proper function as a channel but not creator of these elements. Every Christian is a priest by virtue of his baptism and confirmation and resultant anointing of the Spirit. Out of a renewed sense of this anointing came a new experience of the priesthood of the laity. People wanted to participate in corporate prayer. Often we had to restrain them—there was too much participation for decency and order! Joy is a great fruit of the Spirit, and out of this new experience came floods of joy, so that celebration was the dominant mood of corporate life. As for fellowship, I understand that in some parishes restoration of the "kiss of peace" in the liturgy has aroused the greatest resistance, for people do not want even to shake the hand of their brothers and sisters in Christ. That may be because they do not know them as brothers and sisters. But in the charismatic community, where everyone naturally and spontaneously threw their arms around each other because they saw everyone there as a brother or sister, restoration of the kiss of peace was superfluous.

The point is simply that no external structure will renew Christian life; it simply is not primarily a matter of outer structures. These are very important, no doubt, but they are a derived and not a primary reality. To try to create a sense of mission by exhortation, or a sense of celebration by giving people balloons, or a sense of fellowship by forcing them to shake hands is like sinking a well where there is no water. To dig a well and install a pump is foolish if you are drilling into dry sand. But if the water itself flows powerfully there is no need even to bother to dig a well or buy a pump.

One more thing must be said under this heading. Attempts to renew the church by these techniques are not only unnecessary, since the Spirit longs to do it for us; they are also counterproductive. This is the final implication of our principle that the Spirit is only released through humility and openness. In the last chapter I said as strongly as I knew how that if I were to give you a technique for releasing the Spirit and creating the community I would be a charlatan and a liar. Beware of those who come to you with ideas popping in the brain and blueprints rolled up under their arms! If there were a technique for renewing the church, it would have been used long ago. There have always been clever and energetic people in the church. It is not for want of these qualities that it is not revived; rather, church members have too much talent. There is no possible plan that church people could not put into practice, no technique that they could not employ. And they would do it well—so well that they would begin to be proud of what they were doing and to take credit for their accomplishments. They would begin to say, "Look at us! We're renewing the church—we're carrying out the plan of God." And would be unable to do the one thing necessary: to be broken open and let God's Spirit work.

It is because of an excess of good ideas (and they are *good* ideas) that the church is not renewed. Someone at the national, diocesan, or parish level gets a fine concept of what the church ought to do. There is enough intelligence and energy around to start people to work on it. Others are brought (sometimes forced) in. There is program and activity, and everyone assumes that somehow God's will is being done. Has anyone asked Him?

Some time ago I visited my seminary and was speaking to some of the graduates about what they were doing. The "successful" ones all said about the same thing. They were studying what had to be done in their parish, were taking surveys, planning programs. Full of impressive ideas. But I was suddenly struck by the fact that no one was asking what the Lord wanted done. It would have seemed foolish to inquire, "Is this the Lord's will?" But as Paul reminds us, foolishness is sometimes the wisdom of God. The world is full of good ideas, and I do not deny the merits of any of them. I am just asking whether they are really God's will for that place at that time. In all the whirr of activity everyone is "doing their thing," but no one is seeking the Lord. And this bustle of action may indeed be counterproductive, may make people concentrate so hard on their "thing" that they are unable to be open to the Spirit. If there were fewer good, plausible ideas to try out, maybe they would try harder to seek the Lord. Or maybe when all the ideas have run out, this will break the pride of man enough to open him to the Lord's leading.

Techniques cannot renew the church because a technique is something man does on his own. It builds his pride. Technical expertise is just the opposite of the humble giving of oneself over to God that releases the power of the Spirit. This is not easy to say. I know it goes against the very grain of modern American church life, whether "liberal" or "conservative." But there is a truth here about releasing the Spirit in the lives of men which has been proven in the charismatic movement.

If the church is to be renewed, this must begin where all must begin if they wish to live deeper in the Spirit. It must be still and know that the Lord is God indeed. It must turn from the contemplation of its own plans to a humble waiting on its Lord. It must have the pride burned out of it in a crucible of patience and surrender. It must be open to consider that God's will for His church is not the same as its own. It must learn the lesson of radical openness to God and a complete willingness to "go all the way" with the Lord, even to the point of abandoning its ideas and appearing foolish in the sight of men—even to the point of openness to the gifts of the Spirit. It must learn through pain and patience and prayer what we must all learn in order to be supple in the Spirit. Only then can it be what God wants His church to be: the instrument of His will. If it seeks first the will of God, then all other things—peace and joy, real celebration, fellowship, the excitement of a real apostolate in the world —all will be added unto it in the outpouring of the Spirit that God promises to those who are responsive to Him.

Spiritual Gifts and the Congregation

So far I have spoken on the theoretical level, sketching briefly a new theology of renewal by application to the church of what we have learned about individuals and the building of community. However hard this has been both to say and to accept, I myself have no doubt that it is true. At the more practical level I am less sure, for our experiences have been as yet more limited and the time of testing short. But keeping in mind a real insistence on the temporality of any structures in this time, let me venture the following remarks on how forms of the charismatic movement might relate to the church.

It has already produced several such forms. Perhaps even the creation of Pentecostal sects was a structure of church renewal, if through them God was able to reach His wider church with a deeper experience of the Spirit. But one cannot consider a sectarianism that repudiates the whole of God's church as the vehicle for its renewal. The first form produced by the charismatic movement which may help to revitalize the church is that of spiritually renewed persons. In the early stages of the movement many people were prayed for to receive "the baptism in the Holy Spirit" and set loose on their own. They testify to a renewal of their Christian lives: their faith became deeper, their love increased, they sought more fervently to do the Lord's work. This is the level at which many people define the purpose of the movement—to produce more spiritually alive individuals.

But many pastors will bear me out in the observation that it is often hard for these people to integrate themselves into the life of their congregation. They are apt to meet with hostility. Their zeal can repel their brothers and sisters. The more people around them are turned off, the more zealous they become, until dissension flares and schism erupts. Even those who are more mature find few if any structures in their parish through which they can express their charismatic gifts and grow in the Spirit. Thus even the most seasoned and committed are sometimes forced to choose between loyalty to their church and the need to find a place in which they can live their charismatic experience. Some gradually give up the exercise of spiritual gifts; others leave their churches for charismatic sects. In either case the church suffers, though for the most part seeing it as relief from a nuisance rather than loss of an opportunity.

Thus simply producing charismatically renewed individuals will probably not make a significant change in the church. A few sporadic persons will have little influence on their congregations. Sad but true, the experience seems to be that a small number of Pentecostals more often than not alienates rather than revitalizes a congregation, thereby shutting off its members from further exploring the experience. I have argued that growth in the Spirit cannot take place on an individual basis alone. Its gifts are for the community. Thus unless some community is formed, they will atrophy and the people stagnate.

In light of this it was natural that the charismatic movement, having produced a few spiritually renewed individuals, should take another step: the creation of small prayer groups. This is no doubt the major form the movement has taken to date. All around the nation small groups are being formed in which people can exercise the gifts of the Spirit and deepen their spiritual lives. Often the little group will be the only type of charismatic existence. Sometimes this is by reason of surrounding lack of interest or openness to the movement, sometimes because of the absence of pastoral gifts of leadership and teaching to uphold anything greater. Or at times it is because the group becomes self-satisfied and does not want anything more.

A small group can do a great deal. Within limits it can carry on an effective ministry of prayer and healing. It can serve as a focus for charismatic life. It can certainly meet the needs of its members for fellowship, sharing, and experience. But can it serve to renew the church? Speaking empirically, often it does not. Such groups frequently become unintentionally ingrown and clique-ish; they may adopt subtle customs to inhibit growth, as when a group of women meets during the day when men are not able to come, or takes on a pious jargon which effectively screens out those who differ from the core membership. I have already argued that there are certain built-in difficulties with small groups. Often they are one-sided. If there is a predominance of gifts of prayer or healing, then teaching and pastoral concern may lag, and so on. One or two people who are experiencing psychological difficulties can change the whole temper of the group. In short, it is very difficult for a small prayer group to be the full body of Christ.

It can and should be a cell within that body. Yet a small charismatic group in a parish is apt to have the same problems a few charismatic individuals do. There are no means by which it can channel its experience into the life of the larger whole and have an impact on the congregation. Often the pastor and congregation are precisely willing to tolerate a small group so long as it does *not* make itself felt in the whole congregation. And often the group, realizing that there are no structural means by which it can have input into the congregation, withdraws into itself. Such groups become sects in the midst of churches. They cannot be a vehicle for congregational renewal.

Finally, the movement has taken yet another step, found expression in another form, that of charismatic communities. I have argued indeed that if people are fully open to the Spirit, this will inevitably lead to the formation of Christian community. Gifts of the Spirit are intended for this, and their purpose will be thwarted if it does not happen. Thus small prayer groups should desire to become larger, even at the sacrifice of some of the human comforts of their original cell. For the body of Christ is larger than a small group, and community is necessary if a mature growth in the Spirit is to be achieved. Rather than simply being concerned to meet the needs of their own members, small groups should care about building up the body of Christ—that is, forming Christian communities, where people meet to love and serve each other and to be shaped together into a single body.

Now, how can these charismatic communities function in renewing the church? This question has clearly not yet been fully answered, but a couple of tentative models are being tried. One might be called the "renewal community." This is how most large charismatic communities, such as the one I described in the first chapter, operate, drawing people from several parishes and denominations. The first thing a renewal community does is to provide an experience of the full body of Christ. If the structures of renewal must arise out of the experience of a new life, then these communities serve to provide it. Out of them will evolve new styles of Christian experience and forms of Christian living which can then be transferred to the parish. They also provide a context in which charismatic people can mature in their spiritual lives and from which they can go back into the parishes strengthened for the task of church renewal. One of the reasons that many neo-Pentecostals have both antagonized their fellow church members and become embittered themselves is that they looked on their congregation as both the object of their attempts at renewal and their source of support. It is very hard to draw support from an organization at the same time as one is trying to change it! But the member of a renewal community need not be either aggressive or defensive in his local congregation. Since one receives support from the community, one can live patiently within one's own church waiting for the Lord to work.

The renewal community also provides an example of revitalized Christian life. In it people can witness renewal and not simply discuss it. Instead of arguing over various strategies of church development or change, they can visit such a community and see an awakening of Christianity in progress, and from what they see can learn lessons applicable to their congregations. I have met many people in the movement who had been on various renewal committees in their churches and had become discouraged because all they had seen was debates about renewal. In the charismatic community, instead of arguments about programs they found the *process* of renewal actually going on. Their discouragement turned to hope as they saw these examples of Christian living. Thus the large charismatic community can function as a staging area for revitalization in the local parishes.

Another case of how charismatic community can lead to church renewal might be called the "charismatic parish" model. Here the community becomes a parish. In the Midwest several Roman Catholic bishops have designated certain communities as parishes and have incorporated them into the diocesan structure. Provided with clergy who exercise spiritual gifts, these communities take on the parochial activities of religious instruction, marriage, baptism, and so on. This is parish renewal by fiat and runs the risk that charismatically oriented people will gravitate toward them and leave the bulk of churches untouched by the renewal, thus creating sects in the midst of the church.

Charismatic parishes also arise by the opposite process: a congregation is transformed into a community when all its members become involved in the charismatic movement. The Episcopal Church of the Redeemer in Houston, Texas, is one example of this. It was a dying inner-city church when Fr. Graham Pulkingham took over. Almost all its parishioners had fled the city for the suburbs. Fr. Pulkingham had recently come into the experience of spiritual gifts, and shared this with the leading members of the congregation who remained. Several responded, especially a physician and a lawyer who began to meet regularly with the rector for prayer. Soon the sparsely attended church was charismatic and attracting new people. Led into community, former members in the suburbs began to move back into the city to the area around the church. Now a thriving parish, the Church of the Redeemer is also a charismatic community of people living in the vicinity and providing services to the neighborhood. These combinations of community and parish may point the way toward church renewal, for in them one can experience life in the Spirit and in community in the context of a congregation.

Obviously I do not know how, in the long run, this form of charismatic life will be an agent in renewal, for only God knows how He wants to use the communities He has raised up. But there are several comments one might offer.

1. There is danger of revitalizing only a part of the church. In a renewal community or charismatic parish full renewal of the church—the apostolate, the liturgy, the spiritual gifts—*can* take place. But charismatics, like everyone else, may easily become self-satisfied. Having created a situation in which they are comfortable, they adopt a live-and-let-live attitude under the name of charity. I have argued that the movement must be presented with love and sensitivity and no one coerced into it. But I do believe very strongly (as I'll explain below) that this is *the* movement for the renewal of the church. The reason others have not succeeded is that they simply became one more group in the church, doing its own thing and fragmenting the body rather than renewing it. The liturgical movement became a group for people interested in liturgy, the social apostolate became a social action committee, and so on. The charismatic movement, whether a small prayer group or a large community, must guard itself from becoming just another group for people whose "thing" is speaking in tongues or praying. Its goal is not the creation of groups but a renewal of the body of Christ wherein every "thing"—liturgy, apostolate, prayer, etc.—finds its place. One should not have to choose between concern for social action, worship, and prayer. Every Christian should have a mission, participate in the liturgy, and exercise the gifts God wants him to have. This sounds unreasonable only because we think of each of these as a separate element with its own meetings, leaders, literature, and so forth, and no one has time to do them all. But if one can experience them all together, as one

does in the full community, then there is no need for social action committees or prayer groups since every member of the body has an apostolate or mission suited to his call and a life of prayer within the body. Thus the charismatic movement must not settle for the renewal of a partial church; it must not forever remain one more meeting for people to do a "charismatic thing" divorced from liturgy or mission.

2. In order to help in renewing the body of Christ, people must first experience it. Charismatic communities are indispensable to this end because in them people can learn what that life is like. If the community becomes complete and fully rounded, they can know at first hand the life out of which structures of renewal (a new liturgy, a new apostolate, new pastoral forms, and so on) can and will emerge. Hence I feel this par excellence is the movement for church renewal. It is the one development in which, at least in potential though not invariably in practice, one can *experience* a fully renewed Christian life. It involves concern for a new sense of community, for an apostolate in the world, and for the renewal of worship because it provides the personal experience from which these forms can grow. Therefore, I think the most important service the charismatic community can make to the renewal of the church at this time is to provide an area where life in the full body of Christ can be known.

3. Let me now briefly reiterate that the scaffolding is not the building. In fostering the growth of communities we must remember that we live between the times and not take these structures as permanent. They are, I believe, a necessary stage in the renewal of the whole church. But a stage—not an end. They are vehicles for renewal, not the renewal itself. Like scaffolding, they must be removed when the rebuilt house of God is finished. It is important to build the scaffolding but not in lieu of building the building. It is important that as Pentecostals work on building up charismatic communities this should not

be in order to forsake the church, but for the very sake of the church. If the formation of such groups ever becomes an end in itself, I feel positive that they will have lost their radical obedience and openness to God and their place in His plan, which goes far beyond simply the birth of a few small assemblies in one remote corner of His creation or another.

It is a part of the pain of living between the times that nothing seems clear. For a while there may have to be many groups; we may have to live in several worlds, and equally in a congregation and a charismatic community. Thus we incarnate the suffering of life in this period, for we exist with one foot in what has been and step forward with the other into what is to be. It is easier to live wholly in one sphere, but that would be to deny the call that lies upon those who take up a concern for the church. There is pain associated with growth, and those who undertake to be agents of God in the deeper growth of His church in the Spirit must risk the pain of rejection, of their own impatience, of being pulled in several directions, just as our Lord Himself did when He undertook to be the agent of our salvation.

Having touched upon other problems, I should like now to answer the question, in what sense the charismatic movement is so uniquely the renewal of the church. We have seen how Pentecostalism is a revival of the basic experience of Christianity. We have also seen it as a renewal of Christian community which will naturally lead to a rebirth of worship and discipleship. Two more areas remain to be mentioned briefly: the rebuilding of the foundations and the recreation of the one body of Christ.

I have been at some pains to emphasize that outward forms of Christian existence are derivative and not primary. But there is another sense in which renewal cannot be imposed from the top. The social apostolate or mission and the new liturgy have often not been accepted because there was no foundation for them. Recent attempts to awaken the church assume a firm foundation of Christian belief and experience among its members, and that all that is necessary is to build upon it. Yet this may not be true.

When I was in the seminary I met a man who was one of the leaders of his denomination. He held a national position in which he was concerned about church program. As we talked, it became clear to me that he did not believe any of the basic doctrines of Christianity. Jesus was an irrelevant figure from the past; God was, at most, an inspiring idea. Yet this man was designing programs to renew the church. He served in an important capacity, with responsibility for the life of the church. Now, when people come to the community to receive the release of the Spirit we try to give them some teaching so that they will understand what is happening and avoid certain pitfalls. Even in the case of those who have grown up in the church, we must often begin with the most elementary teachings of the gospel: the Good News of God's love, the place of Jesus, the way we enter into relationship with Him and appropriate that love.

It is not my wish to judge anyone's heart or mind. But programs for renewal must be built on something, and what I am suggesting is that often, in those responsible for administering them as well as those who ought to benefit from them, there is no such foundation. Programs imposed from above will not invigorate the life of the congregation because they will not really touch it. Thus I believe that any movement for renewal must begin as the charismatic movement does, by laying again the foundation of basic Christian teaching and experience. Only in such ground can the structures of renewal be firmly anchored.

Second, there must be a renewal of *the one body of Christ.* Everyone recognizes the ecumenical movement as one of the great movements of the Spirit in the church today. But the same principles apply. Structural ecumenism which does not grow out of a genuine ecumenical life will produce only empty wineskins, just as patterns of renewal that do not grow out of a renewed life will themselves have no vitality. The charismatic movement is *the* ecumenical movement, not because it is creating structural realignments (it isn't), but because it is bringing into being a new sense of the common life of the people of God. So also true ecumenical forms must arise out of a new ecumenical life.

Let me give you one example. Minnesota has many people of the conservative Protestant tradition. Even though—or maybe because—the state is heavily Roman Catholic, these churches have been violently anti-Catholic. While I was in a charismatic community there, evangelical pastors who had been turned off by the Pentecostals in their own churches received the gifts of the Spirit through this community. Two or three of these men stood up in the community and did public penance for what they had been taught and what they themselves had previously said about the Catholic church. In fact, I first learned about the community from a classical Pentecostal minister in the state who himself went to it because the gifts of the Spirit operated more freely there than in his own congregation. Several classical Pentecostals came to the community to go through our teaching series about spiritual gifts.

People from the Catholic tradition were humble and open enough to be led into something they had previously associated only with Protestants, while Protestants were humble and open enough to seek public forgiveness for what they had said against their Catholic brothers. Pentecostals were humble and open enough to learn new things about Pentecostal gifts from their traditional enemies and detractors. So are God's people brought together. The full body of Christ is neither Catholic, Reformed, nor Pentecostal; it is simply the body of Christ. As each group becomes more open to it, the Spirit works to purge them of their cultural accretions and one-sidedness and brings to light forgotten aspects of their own traditions. Thus God's people are drawn together, not by coercion or structural manipulation, but by the pull of the common life of Christ.

In this way the charismatic thrust accomplishes what other movements have sought to achieve. It is not simply a renewal of spiritual gifts, although that is its distinctive feature. But it also revitalizes Christian discipleship, worship, fellowship, and ecumenical relations.

The Glorious Power of the Sons of God

Why does God want His church renewed? Not so that it can rest content with itself, but so that it can be an agent in His plan to fill all things with Himself. Paul says that those who excel in spiritual gifts must excel in building up the body of Christ. As the body is filled, the Spirit goes forth into the world; as God does little things, people's faith is built up, and as their faith is built up, He is able to do even greater things through them. In the body of Christ one sees the corporate life of man filled with the Spirit and submitted to the Lord of the cosmos—one catches a glimpse of the Kingdom of God, a foretaste of its presence. It is no longer an idle dream with which men titillate their imaginations, or a burden we feel we must struggle and strain under. As a seed grows by its own nature into a tree, or as yeast by its particular power raises the dough, so the Kingdom comes by its own dynamic, that of the Spirit at work in the world. Paul writes: "We all, with an open face, beholding and reflecting the glory of the Lord, are being transformed into his likeness by degrees. This is done by the Lord who is the Spirit" (2 Cor. 3:18). As we behold the Lord, as we experience Him and are open to Him, we are transformed. Not for our own sake, but so that as individuals and as corporate members we may also reflect Him, and others can behold Him. As they in turn are transformed, still others will know His presence. So the living image of Christ is brought into the world, and the Kingdom comes.

Concern for renewal of the church is not a sign of lack of caring for the world and its problems, but rather arises precisely because one is concerned about them. To build up the body of Christ is to hasten the day when it is a finer instrument for God to use in the renewal of creation. Even the church is not an end in itself but an agent in recreating the cosmos by filling it with the presence of God.

Paul writes that the Spirit that lives within us is the same mighty power that raised Jesus from the dead. Just meditate on that for a minute! The Spirit within us is the very power of God Himself, victorious even over our last enemy, death. Think of what would happen if we really believed that there dwelt within us a force stronger than death. The disciples healed the sick and even raised the dead because they knew with such absolute awareness that the power within them was that of Jesus' victory over death. Individual saints throughout the ages have looked the fiercest evils in the eye and have borne them down, because they knew they could rely on the strength of one who has victory over all forces of evil. Think of how our lives would change if we really believed in that power—how our religion would come alive, if the strongest force in the universe were released into our active experience. And consider how the purpose of God would progress if there were not just a few individual saints but whole communities of people at work with the power that death itself cannot destroy.

Now that we come to an end, I ask you to think about the fact that there is within every Christian the force of Almighty God Himself. We can all release that Spirit more than we do now. If we gather together into a single body, each with his or her avenue to the Spirit, the increase in power by multiplication will be enormous—geometric. The body of the Lord will be formed and ready for work. I cannot predict what will happen. Perhaps the blind will receive their sight in the midst of your congregation. Maybe the lame will leap for joy in the aisles of your church. Maybe the poor and imprisoned will hear a good word from your pulpit. But whatever else happens, I promise you that the light of God will blaze forth, and you will hasten the day when the earth shall be filled with the glory of God as the waters fill up the sea.

Q. You're too hard on the programs for renewal. I have seen parishioners become alive and involved through the chance to participate more in worship or social action. These things give people a chance to express their Christianity, and that must lead to renewal.

A. Yes, it does lead to renewal if the life is already there. These forms express the new life, but they cannot create it *de novo.* Many have found these new forms don't renew the church, because they have expected them to create a new life and they didn't. But if there is a deep Christian life in your congregation, then these new forms can encourage its expression in exciting ways.

Q. Do you really expect everyone to become involved in the charismatic movement?

A. No. I don't really expect everyone to become involved in it as a separate thing. I do expect that someday all churches will be charismatic again as they were at the beginning; that is, the exercise of spiritual gifts and the importance of the Spirit will find their place in the life of the church and the individual. When that time comes every Christian will be charismatic, and there will be no need for a separate charismatic movement.

Q. When you talk about this renewal of the Spirit and this feeling in a large group and everyone getting the Spirit of God and hugging one another and being joyful, it sounds a little overemotional to me. Comment on that. How do you prove it's an authentic experience and not just emotion?

A. This question always comes up. I don't know how I can prove it is an "authentic experience" rather than "just emotion." The way one knows spiritual gifts are genuine is by the fruit they bear. I have been in assemblies where there is a great deal of charismatic flash, and yet week after week the spirit of the group is one of depression or resentment. Something is wrong there. An authentic religious experience involves the whole person: mind, body, soul, spirit, emotion, and what-have-you. Therefore it must have an emotional element, for feelings are part of the whole person. If a prayer meeting were just an academic discussion it would not be a full religious experience, for it would not touch the whole person but only the mind. If an experience is only emotional it won't be complete either. That's what I meant before about it having to bear fruit in the intellectual and moral life—the person will learn new things about God and man and bear new fruit. I think we are afraid of the emotions, yet they are part of life. A full religious experience will have its emotional side just as a full marriage or a true aesthetic experience will.

Q. Should teaching always take place before people become permanent members of a group? Does the charismatic experience have to occur in the community?

A. I think so. In our community we do not pray for anyone to exercise spiritual gifts unless there has been preparation (particularly teaching) and the opportunity for these people to join a community in which they can grow and participate. In the early days of the renewal people were prayed for with no preparation and let loose on their own. As I said earlier, it's a miracle more did not get into trouble. We've learned something since then about how to avoid many problems created by this haphazard method of bringing people into charismatic experience. Unless the circumstances are really extraordinary, I don't think anyone should be prayed for to exercise spiritual gifts until they have a sound foundation on which to build their new life in the Spirit—until they've made a responsible commitment to Jesus Christ and have had good teaching on the nature and purpose of spiritual gifts. If the person is not going to be involved in a community, if he just wants to exercise these gifts for his own private benefit, or even to satisfy a wide-ranging curiosity or need for power, his spiritual growth will be thwarted. Therefore I think the experience of spiritual gifts ought to take place in community. Obviously persons can pray in the Spirit or come into the gift of tongues outside of a community meeting. But their spiritual life ought to be lived, in part, in community.

Q. On occasion the hierarchy or structure of the church has allowed only a small renewal or has put the movement down. What happens when the church refuses to be renewed? What would you suggest for someone in the charismatic movement to do when he runs up against this type of thing in his denomination or local parish? Should he leave the church?

A. This may be less and less of a problem. More and more churches and denominations are losing their opposition to Pentecostal experience. But a particular church or diocese may go against this general trend and (against Paul's injunction) "forbid speaking in tongues." I don't think a person should leave the church. The scandal these acts of schism give to the charismatic renewal is very serious. I think Pentecostal people must walk circumspectly and be sure they do not give offense out of a lack of wisdom or charity. If the sheer fact of being a Pentecostal is an offense and they are excommunicated, then they have to leave. But then the judgment is on the church and not on them. A person should not voluntarily leave his church. He should join a charismatic community where he can get support and grow in the Spirit, and at the same time remain in his own church. The act of schism gives great scandal to the charismatic renewal.

Q. Some of us want to follow up on what you've said. Where can we go? *127028 SpRINGWooD, C ALif.*

A. I'd suggest visiting various charismatic communities and prayer meetings.* Visit a classical Pentecostal church, too. I think I have given you some idea of what to look for, and also what to watch out for. Be as open as possible and you can gain something from almost any kind of group. Just remember one thing—you don't have to "do like they do"! Resist any pressure on you to do things exactly as you see them in whatever kind of group you visit. There are many different styles of charismatic life developing in the present.

---

*A directory of Roman Catholic groups is available from the Communications Center, P.O. Box 12, Notre Dame, Indiana 46556; of Episcopalian groups from the Episcopal Charismatic Fellowship, 100 Colorado Boulevard, Denver, Colorado 80206; of Presbyterian groups from the Presbyterian Charismatic Communion, 428 Northwest 34th Street, Oklahoma City, Oklahoma 73118.

74 75 76 77 10 9 8 7 6 5 4 3 2 1